Dedication

This book is in memory and honor of our son, Nathan, who taught me how to live life to the full and is dedicated to my husband, Dave, and our daughter, Ashley, whose love and support help make the dream of publishing this book a reality.

Nathan
Still a Gift of God

Teresa C. Sours

Nathan Still a Gift of God

Copyright © 2010 by Tersa Sours

ISBN 978-0-615-40671-8

Published By:
Isaiah 61 Ministries
2267 Mount Torrey Road
Lyndhurst, VA 22952
(540) 487-4619
isaiah61@ntelos.net

No portion of this book may be reprinted without written permission from the author.

Printed By:
Campbell Copy Center
755 Cantrell Ave
Harrisonburg, Virginia

Table of Contents

Introduction	vii
Background	ix
1 An Uncertain Pregnancy	1
2 Our Miracle Baby	11
3 He's Finally Home!	23
4 Our New Norm	31
5 Making Some Progress	45
6 Victories and Challenges	51
7 Off to School	59
8 Season of Preparation	69
9 Life's Never Dull	77
10 Season of Testing	83
11 Growing Health Concerns	93
12 No Other Option	101
13 Preparing for Transplant	111
14 Our Worst Nightmare	121
15 Our Son's Funeral	131
16 Life Goes On	135
17 Back to School	141
18 Journey Into Grief	147
19 God at Work	153
20 The First Thanksgiving	159
21 The First Birthday	163
22 Our First Christmas	167
23 Call to Ministry	175
24 The Challenges Continue	179
25 Change is Inevitable	185
26 Our First Easter	191
27 In Memory Of	197
28 One Year Anniversary	201
29 More New Beginnings	209
30 Time Goes On	217
31 2001 To Present	221
32 What About Today?	227
Photos	237
Appendix and End Notes	243

Nathan Still a Gift of God

Introduction

Most of what you are about to read has been taken from my personal journals. Actually, three different sets of journals: my daughter's, which I started when she was just a baby; my son's, which I started before he was even born at the prompting of God; and my own personal journals, which evolved out of the first two. To help set the stage, here is the opening entry of Nathan's journal, which I began while I was still pregnant with him and facing a very uncertain future. As I share this and other entries, I trust you are able to get past the simple language and often times poor grammar and hear my mother's heart as I struggled to come to terms with the unfolding of the story of *Nathan: Still a Gift of God*.

> *My Most Precious Nathan,*
>
> *Eventually this book will end up being a daily account of your life, your activities, your achievements with added tidbits from your mother—my thoughts and feelings. But for starters, I want to share my life with you in the days and weeks before you were born. I hope that one day you will appreciate and understand the fact that you are a miracle...a blessing from above. And I also want to give you some insight as to what we, your parents and family, have been through physically, mentally, emotionally, and most of all spiritually, both during and after pregnancy with you. I thank God every day for what He's done for you (and continues to do) and for us. The doctor's can't say for sure what the future holds but then who can? I just know that whatever it is, God will see us through. I hope that one day you'll come to know that too, and also know that Mommy and Daddy love you very, very much and will always be here for you no matter what...*

Nathan Still a Gift of God

Background

Before I begin telling Nathan's story, I thought it important to understand my (our) life (lives) leading up to the events of 1991. In 1987, I was a newlywed, a full-time student, and employed full-time as an accounts receivable clerk. Life was very full. My husband Dave and I purchased and moved into our first home just in time to celebrate our first wedding anniversary.

On the evening of Thursday, September 24, I received a phone call from my mom. She had been developing pictures, a new hobby of hers, and wanted me to come up for a visit and see her latest batch of pictures. I said I'd love to, but I was too busy with homework and things around the house.

It wasn't too long before I received another phone call from someone who lived just down the mountain from my parents. He said there had been an accident and my mother and youngest brother were being taken to the local hospital. I asked if they were okay. He hesitated but finally said, "It's pretty bad." I quickly hung up, screamed for Dave, and he and I rushed to the hospital.

Long story short, because I couldn't (wouldn't) come see her, my mom got a ride with my brother who was on his way to see his girlfriend. Several miles from the house, they met an on-coming vehicle on a curve. There was a head-on collision, and my mother died on impact. My brother suffered a broken neck and was hospitalized for a couple weeks. In an instant, our lives were changed forever.

Being the oldest of four children, I felt a strong sense of responsibility to fill in the gaps my mom's death left, especially with my younger sister who was only fourteen at the time. I couldn't keep all the plates spinning and eventually began dropping classes until I dropped out of college all together.

A maternal switch was flipped somewhere inside me following mom's death, and Dave and I decided to start a family. I became pregnant only to have a miscarriage at fourteen weeks of pregnancy. After the suggested waiting period, we became pregnant again. This time we gave birth to a beautiful, healthy baby girl, Rebecca "Ashley" Sours. Some of the gaps mom's death had left began to be filled. A year-and-a-half later we decided we'd like to have another child. Our third pregnancy ended in miscarriage at two months, certainly not as devastating as the first, but nevertheless another loss.

We quickly became pregnant for a fourth time and that's where *Nathan: Still a Gift of God* begins.

All scripture references are taken from the New International Version of the Bible unless otherwise noted.

An Uncertain Pregnancy

Initial Journal Entries:

April 13: *I confirmed with a home pregnancy test what I already knew in my heart.*

April 24: *A doctor's test agreed with my own. The queasiness followed within a matter of weeks. Ashley, 1 ½ years old at the time, would pat my tummy and say, "Baby in there." She would then pat her own and say, "Baby in Ashley's tummy." Cute!*

May 19: *I felt a "fluttering" in my tummy, one of the most wonderful sensations of pregnancy.*

May 31: *We heard a very muffled heart beat.*

June 8: *Out of necessity, I showed up at a family function in maternity clothes letting everyone know the good news! The baby's movements grew stronger and more frequent. I had forgotten how wonderful it feels to be pregnant!*

July 3: *We heard a very definite heart beat. The doctor said it sounded like a girl! How exciting!*

July 18: *Dave and I both felt the baby's kicks with our hands on my tummy. A personal note to baby: I hope one day you'll enjoy and appreciate these very simple pleasures in life.*

July 27: *We could see the baby moving and bumping around in my tummy. This was a very active child!*

Everything was going so well, so normal, until August 7 when we went in for a routine ultrasound. We were about twenty weeks into the pregnancy at this point, and our biggest concern of the day was whether or not to ask the sex of the baby. Boy, were we in for a surprise! As Dr. Thompson was performing the ultrasound, he was pointing out the different organs. When he got to the bladder and kidneys, even I could see something wasn't quite right. In comparison to the other organs, they were huge. I asked several questions but really didn't get direct answers. Dr. Thompson took many measurements and made notations. When he was finished, he said to get dressed and we would talk in his office.

Once seated in his office, we discovered that he suspected our baby had a urinary blockage. The blockage was preventing the baby from peeing and creating the amniotic fluid needed for fetal development. Since the urine was not able to escape the body, it had backed up into the bladder and kidneys causing the entire urinary system to be stretched and enlarged, which was what we were seeing on the ultrasound. This problem was not totally uncommon for little boys. (We now knew we were having a little boy!) When the blockage develops after birth, it typically isn't a problem. When it develops in utero, it's a big problem. Being human, we naturally assumed there was some mistake or at least things couldn't be as dismal as they were portrayed.

Dr. Thompson was able to schedule an appointment at the University of Virginia Hospital (U.Va.) to confirm his findings. And Dr. Ferguson did just that—confirmed it! This just couldn't be happening! This is the kind of stuff that happens to someone else, not us! You tell yourself maybe it isn't all that bad, refusing to accept the fact your baby is in trouble. But the situation was bad. Very bad. The blockage was preventing our baby from creating the amniotic fluid that he needed for movement, growth, and most importantly, lung development. A secondary concern was the damage the

1 An Uncertain Pregnancy

blockage was causing and had already caused to the entire urinary system. We were given choices.

We could do nothing, and the chances of our baby living were less than ten percent. He'd probably be stillborn, or if he did manage to live, there would probably not be enough lung development to support life. If he did live, he would probably have deformities in his extremities because of the weight of my body pressing in on him, as well as possible brain damage. We could abort, which we never REALLY considered but sadly was an attractive alternative compared to what we were facing. It would be so simple to just start over.

Our third option was an experimental procedure. First, we would have a test performed, much like amnio, where urine would be drawn from the baby's bladder to see if certain elements were present in order to know if the kidneys were still functioning or not. If they were, we would then have a surgical procedure whereby a catheter or shunt would be placed in the baby's bladder to allow the urine to drain and create the amniotic fluid. The procedure itself carried with it the danger of spontaneous miscarriage, plus there was no way to know the extent of damage already done to the lungs, brain, or extremities. To make matters worse, we had to make a decision by the next morning!

Dave and I were overwhelmed with the discoveries of the day! I'd always wondered what I'd do in a situation like this. Now, unfortunately, I was finding out. We were devastated, heartbroken! We shed countless tears. I was very angry! Why me?! Why my child?! That night I couldn't sleep. I finally got up and grabbed my Bible and prayed for words of encouragement. I prayed for something, anything. I opened my Bible at random, and God gave me Luke 10:19. It was Jesus talking. *I have given you authority to overcome all the power of the enemy; nothing will harm you.* This was the first time and these are the first words where I KNEW God was speaking directly to me! And those words really lifted my spirit! We can overcome this! The next day I was replacing bookmarks that Ashley had taken out of my Bible and found myself staring at Luke 11:9 *Ask and it will be given to you; seek and you will find; knock and it will be opened to you.* For the first time since hearing the news, I felt hope for our horrible situation. Further down, it talks of a father giving his child what he asks and how much more our Father in Heaven can give us. I was still very upset, but I had the knowledge that God can touch and heal and give us the baby we wanted so badly. And if for some reason things go differently, I knew He was in control, would see us through, and would take us on to whatever His plan is for our little family. We decided to have the test done.

Dr. Ferguson called Thursday morning. Our appointment was scheduled for 8:30 on the morning of Ashley's second birthday, of all days! It was a horrible experience! They used several needles to numb my tummy and then inserted a larger one to inject fluid around the baby so they could have working space. Then, they finally drew fluid off our baby's bladder. I felt so physically ill during the test! It was awful! I was sore and tired and then had to wait the whole weekend before we'd have the results on Monday. Dave's mom, Peggy, pampered us all weekend. What would we do without her?

Monday, the twelfth, was a very anxious day spent waiting for the doctor to call—he didn't. We didn't get the results until Tuesday, and three of the four tests were poor for kidney function. I lost it again! I was so depressed! So angry! Now, we had to decide whether to go ahead with the in utero surgery knowing there probably wasn't enough

… kidney function to support the pregnancy, even if we did have it done. Ashley spent the day with grandparents so I could have time to think.

Phillip Hunt, my dad's pastor at Wayne Hills Baptist Church, called. We had been on the prayer list at their church, and he was calling to check on us. I had never met the man, but I asked him how could we make a decision like this and how could we know it's the right one? He said once we make our decision, we will have peace. I couldn't imagine having "peace" in the middle of the worst time of my life! Not even the death of my mother could compare. She was gone, and I could do nothing but accept it. But this…such intense pressure as we made life and death decisions for our baby.

Pastor Hunt also suggested we seek counsel with someone who had a similar experience. My cousin Vanessa immediately came to mind. Her baby Matthew had been born with kidney disease and was now on dialysis and a breathing machine. (Most likely there was not a genetic component with Matthew's and our baby's conditions. Matthew was dealing with diseased kidneys, while our baby's kidney problems were caused by the physical problem of a blockage.) I called her and asked if I could come and talk with her. She, of course, agreed. I was absolutely overwhelmed at first with all the medical equipment in their home and especially in Matthew's room. But as I spent time with her, little Matthew and his nurse, I could see how happy he was in spite of his medical condition. When I left, I knew I could never abort my baby, no matter what problems he might have. In fact, I knew we needed to do everything within our means to give our baby every chance regardless of what the tests indicated. Then with God's help, I could accept and handle whatever would be because He gives us nothing we can't bear. An unexplainable peace fell on me. I was actually smiling as I drove to meet Dave for lunch and tell him of my meeting with Vanessa and Matthew and of my decision to have the surgical procedure. He agreed with me, and I left for home to make the arrangements to have the catheter placed despite the terrible odds. The catheter was the one and only thing we had to give our baby at least some chance of survival. The rest was up to God.

God then gave me Philippians 4:4-7:

> *Rejoice in the Lord always. I will say it again: Rejoice! Let your gentleness be evident to all. The Lord is near. Do not be anxious about anything, but in everything, by prayer and petition, with thanksgiving, present your requests to God. And the peace of God, which transcends all understanding, will guard your hearts and your minds in Christ Jesus.*

I knew we had God's approval in our decision. I memorized the passage from Philippians to get me through this procedure, especially in light of the terrible experience of the last! The surgery took place on August 16. It was uncomfortable to say the least...more needles...another big needle. (The larger needle remained in my tummy and is what Dr. Ferguson worked through, inserting the instruments through it to place the catheter inside the baby's bladder.) They had trouble because our baby was so small and turned wrong, but the doctor was able to get the catheter into the baby's bladder and see an immediate decompression—a good sign. I had to spend the night in the hospital for observation and to monitor our baby's condition. None of us slept much that night. I had a very sleepless night in the hospital. At home, Ashley woke up in

1 An Uncertain Pregnancy

the night wanting me, which made me feel good (and bad!) so of course poor daddy didn't get much sleep either.

On August 23, we were to find out if the catheter was working and if there was any evidence of kidney function. I dreaded this ultrasound more than I did the procedure to place the catheter! I was so afraid of what they'd find. I was so afraid of more bad news, and to be honest I wasn't sure if I could take any more. We had a long wait in the doctor's office. Much to the doctor's surprise, the ultrasound showed almost a normal amount of fluid around the baby! A definite sign of kidney function! We were ecstatic! Dr. Ferguson told us that he performed the procedure more for our peace of mind than the possibility it might work. There was only one explanation: GOD!!! FAITH!!! PRAYER!!! MIRACLE!!! I was grinning from ear to ear; actually giggling! There was one problem: there was some fluid inside the baby's abdominal cavity, possibly from a tear in the bladder, but for now we were in a much better position than before. Dave and I celebrated with breakfast at Shoney's! We were absolutely floating on air with thankfulness, happiness, and hope.

On the twenty-ninth, we had a routine OB visit locally. Once the OB heard our pregnancy story, he wanted to do an ultrasound for his own curiosity. I didn't mind at all. It gave me another chance to confirm our baby was doing ok, which he was, with plenty of fluid surrounding him. We also had a follow-up visit with Dr. Ferguson. There was even more fluid than two weeks earlier! Dr. Ferguson said that I "must have angels sitting on my shoulders." And today the baby didn't have his legs crossed; we were definitely having a little boy! In response to the doctor's comment about "angels on my shoulders," Peggy got me a gold angel pin to wear, which I did quite often, reminding me of what God had done for us.

The baby and my belly were growing by leaps and bounds. Dave and I went out to dinner to celebrate our fifth anniversary, and my belly was so big we had to get the couple seated behind us to get up and move their table back so I could get my belly under our table! At my next OB visit, I discovered I had gained nine pounds in three weeks! We were also able to see our baby sucking his thumb and fingers on the ultrasound. Precious!

The beginning of October brought a bit of a scare. I ended up in the ER twice with premature labor! They were able to stop it with medication, which I would continue to take until it was time for him to be born. The baby had enough working against him without adding prematurity on top of it. This pregnancy was proving to be very tiring—mentally, emotionally, as well as physically. This may very well be our last.

Over the course of the next month, we had almost weekly ultrasounds to check the progress and condition of the baby. This provided ample opportunity for various family members to tag along and see the baby. We also began to discuss delivery options and dates. I had to let go of my hopes for a vaginal delivery in exchange for a scheduled cesarean section, which would be less stressful for the baby.

By mid-November, we as a family had decided on a name for our unborn child. Ashley decided on the name "Sister" for her baby brother and also informed us she planned to paint his toenails pink! Although we were certain he would love that, Dave and I decided on the name "Nathaniel David." David, of course, after his father, and Nathaniel, meaning "gift of God," which we thought very fitting with the way he had beaten the odds so far. We were optimistic but nervous about the final outcome.

On November 18, Dr. Ferguson took us by surprise

1 An Uncertain Pregnancy

when he wanted to do an amnio to test for lung maturity. Depending on the results, it could mean a c-section in as early as a few days! It sent me into a panic. It turned out that the lungs were not quite ready which suited me just fine. I was not ready mentally, emotionally, or physically for the birth of this baby. Ready or not, time was running out. November 30 was the last day for the premature labor meds. I was in a major nesting mode! I was excited, nervous, worried, and tired. I was also feeling guilty over all the times I left Ashley for doctor's appointments and in order to have some much needed rest. But when I was with her, I was tired and grouchy. Talk about guilt! Hopefully we could soon put all this behind us and return to some sort of a normal life.

Nathan Still a Gift of God

Our Miracle Baby

Just before midnight on December 1, 1991, the contractions started. They were seven to ten minutes apart and Dave started getting an upset tummy, reminiscent of when Ashley was born. We already had a 9 a.m. appointment the next morning to test again for lung maturity. In light of a night of contractions, we headed off to our appointment with suitcase and camera in hand just in case. While we were in the waiting room, Dave said he had a dream several nights before. We were in a very similar room and the doctor came in and said, "Today's the day!" Well guess what? It was!!! The ultrasound that morning showed hardly any amniotic fluid around the baby again and an increase in the fluid in Nathan's tummy. Dr. Ferguson said the baby needed to be born now. I hadn't eaten anything because of the contractions. They scheduled the c-section for 3 p.m. that afternoon.

Grandma Peggy came over for the big occasion and to be supportive. Dave was holding together surprisingly well so far. I was starving and thirsty. Dr. Ferguson kept tabs on us while munching on peanut M & Ms! The surgery was under way a little after three. All the doctors and nurses were very nice, and many had a sense of humor that made the whole thing a lot easier. The operating room was full of people, mostly because they were expecting a very sick little baby to be born.

Once the surgery began, things moved quickly. At one point, I thought Dave wasn't going to get gowned up in time. Neither of us could see the actual procedure because of the little curtain, but we got a blow-by-blow account from the anesthesiologist. Dr. Ferguson said, "Head's out!" We held our breath and prayed. There was complete silence as

Nathan Still a Gift of God

we waited to hear the all important scream, which would be a good initial indication that the lungs were okay. We heard them suctioning his nose and mouth. Then, "One shoulder's out!" Then the most beautiful, wonderful sound of our baby's crying filled the room! One of the doctors said, "Nothing wrong with those lungs!" Our baby Nathan was born on December, 2, 1991, at 3:55 p.m., weighing a hefty eight pounds eleven ounces and was nineteen inches long.

Dave and I fell apart with joy! We shed tears of happiness and thankfulness. There are just no words to describe how we felt at that moment! Praise God!!! They whisked Nathan by us for a quick look. He was such a pretty (or should I say handsome?!) pink baby with a chubby little face and fuzzy black hair! Then it was off to the NICU (Neonatal Intensive Care Unit) for Nathan to have a thorough exam of his medical condition. I was taken to recovery, while Dave and others got to go down and see Nathan. I didn't get to see him until later that night.

The initial reports from the doctors: they couldn't find the catheter—they weren't sure if it was inside Nathan or me or where it might be; there was a piece of tissue where the catheter had been in his tummy that looked like a little piece of sausage—they weren't sure if it was a piece of fatty tissue, bladder, bowel, abdominal lining, or what and there could be a potential problem if it were bowel; they were not sure where the blockage was yet; they were not sure of the level of kidney function; but the lungs were fine! And there was no sign of brain damage, handicapping conditions or any other significant concerns other than those stated above! We had ourselves a little miracle baby!

I slept very little that night. By morning, my diet had advanced from ice chips to clear liquids, juices, Jell-O, tasteless broth, and sherbet. M-m-m! I was very sore and

2 Our Miracle Baby

moving very slowly. But I got to hold Nathan for the first time! A mother's joy! Even if it meant I only scooped him up and held him over his bed. All the wires and tubes attached to his little body prevented anything beyond that. It was very uncomfortable and unnatural but still a wonderful feeling to hold my baby boy!

Dave and his mom brought Ashley over for a visit. I had left her yesterday morning telling her I'd be back later. Then there began a steady stream of family members coming to welcome the newest member to the family.

Nathan's first day of life consisted of a partial scan of his renal system followed by surgery as soon as an operating room became available. The doctors found the catheter and removed it from his bladder. The piece of mystery tissue turned out to be just fatty tissue, and they tucked it back in. They also performed a vesicostomy where they created an opening just below Nathan's belly button that would constantly drain urine from the bladder directly into his diaper since the blockage prevented him from peeing naturally on his own. (They did not think it in Nathan's best interest to remove the blockage yet.) The opening on his tummy looked like a pair of lips and was about the same size. They said he did well during surgery, but Nathan was really groggy from the anesthesia. He was also hooked up to lots of tubes and wires: he was on a ventilator, there was a tube in his nose for draining his tummy, which was one of the worst for me to see, an IV, a tube in his naval for drawing blood, a catheter, breathing monitors, as well as wires to monitor his temperature and his heart rate. Need I say more?! It was quite a bit for a mother to absorb.

By December 4, merely forty-eight hours into life, Nathan was still zonked. It was pitiful to see him laying there! It broke my heart! They began weaning him off the ventilator and took him completely off by afternoon. That left him so hoarse that when he'd cry there was no noise. There is nothing worse than a baby's silent cry! His little lips were so dry. The tape from the ventilator tube left nasty marks on his face when they removed it. I did the only thing a mother could do in a situation like this: I cried! And oh how I cried!

I actually got to sit and hold Nathan—pure joy! And more tears. I felt so cheated out of the natural mother-child situation. I was so angry and upset about all that he was having to go through! Dave and Ashley came over later and Daddy got to hold his little boy for the first time—more joy! Ashley seemed to be taking in everything—particularly fascinated by my incision. She sang "Jingle Bells" at the top of her lungs as we walked down the hallway.

On the evening of December 5, I left the hospital without my baby. I was happy and sad all at the same time. I was anxious to get home to Dave and Ashley, but I hated leaving Nathan behind. I spent most of the day with him stroking his hair, arms, feet and hands. What a beautiful baby! And he was so content under the circumstances. They removed the tube from his belly button as well as the breathing monitors. He was looking better all the time. Dave came over for a quick visit with Nathan before taking me home. A quick visit because Ashley was at home with the flu. One of the hardest things I ever had to do was leave him at the hospital under someone else's care.

I was up much of the night with Ashley as she battled the flu. I was so glad to be home, but I was still not feeling tip-top. I spent the next morning with Ashley in between phone calls and pumping breast milk. This whole thing hadn't been easy for Ashley either. All those months of a difficult pregnancy, then I leave and don't come back home for days.

2 Our Miracle Baby

Oh, the mother guilt! Either way I went I had guilt—with Ashley, I felt guilty for not being with Nathan; with Nathan, I felt guilty for not being with Ashley.

I didn't get back over to the hospital until late afternoon. They had started giving Nathan a bottle, first with sterile water, then they tried the breast milk that I had pumped. He was doing fairly well. I got to hold him, rock him and give him a bottle! It was beyond words! I watched him as he took the nipple in his mouth and swished it around a little. He took a little suck and got this puzzled look on his face. Then his eyes got big, and he emptied it in no time!

A current renal scan showed he had 2/3 function in his right kidney and only a 1/3 in his left. His creatinine level was rising much slower now and could actually be leveling off. (Creatinine has to do with the metabolism of creatine, a protein, which is typically removed by the kidneys. Creatinine levels are monitored through blood work and one of the things used to determine kidney function—the lower the number, the better the function.) Also because of the extensive kidney damage, he was unable to concentrate his urine, so he was peeing way too much. His doctor made a comment that Nathan was the first successful in utero drainage they had seen. When I got home from my afternoon at the hospital, Ashley met me with, "Mommy, you come back!" Ouch!

I began feeling better and of course over did it. Ashley was still sick and fussy, and now that I was home, she wouldn't let me out of her sight. I couldn't drive for two weeks which meant I had to rely on others—not an easy thing to do for someone who is self-sufficient! But I had no choice—Nathan needed breast milk delivered daily. Because of his medical condition, they said breast milk would be best for him. They loaned me an electric breast pump (a double-pumper actually!) to make it "easier" for me.

On December 7, I had another moment of mother joy—I got to try to nurse Nathan for the first time. He didn't actually nurse that well, but it was a joy nevertheless. The nurses reported that he really enjoyed eating—they knew my baby better than I did at this point. They said he was doing so well that they were going to start reducing his fluid intake from the IV and see if he could make up the difference with the bottle. I think they allowed me to nurse Nathan more for my benefit than for his. Of course, there was no way to measure how much he ate when he nursed, and keeping track of input was very important at this point. Plus, nursing took a lot more energy for Nathan, and he would tire easily and fall asleep rather than eat as he should. Something so simple and natural had become so complicated!

The next day was Sunday, and we skipped church (we were attending the one-room church I grew up in at the time), slept late then went to see Nathan. What a difference a day can make! Yesterday he had a fever, today he was fine, his creatinine was down to 1.9, he was peeing less, and he nursed much better this time! Dave got to feed him a bottle. We were on top of the world! We even got to change our first messy diaper. The simple and natural acts of feeding and changing your baby—make that "beautiful" baby—gave us both such a thrill!

Then on Monday, even more progress was made. Nathan got to move to a much simpler bed without all the gizmos and gadgets. And by Tuesday, his creatinine was down even more to 1.7. While Dave and I were there, we went through our usual routine of my taking a turn at nursing and then Dave following up with a bottle. When it came time for us to leave, Nathan fussed and then just plain cried. Ol' softie couldn't bear to leave him like that, so we stayed and I rocked him and gave him some more bottle until he calmed down. I couldn't wait to have my baby home!

By Thursday, he was off the glucose IV completely, and his creatinine was 1.5! But now, Dave was sick with whatever Ashley had earlier. When it rains, it pours! By Friday, I was not doing well mentally or emotionally. Here's what I journaled to Nathan:

> *Mommy's really down today! I feel so cheated out of your first few days and weeks of life! But yet I'm so thankful for what we have. You'll soon discover your mother's a basket case sometimes. Feeling so helpless not being able to drive and needing others for transportation.*

And I wrote about my visit with him that day:

> *Mommy just held you and rocked you and admired your beautiful little face! It felt so good!!!*

I then journaled to Ashley:

> *Mommy's having a bad day. Feel like everything's closing in on me. Don't know how much more I can take...when will it all end...feeling sorry for myself... miss my independence in driving...mommy needs to get it together for your sake...Mommy loves you sweetie!! I know you've been neglected lately but you're still loved with all our hearts!!!*

On my visit Saturday the 14, Nathan's creatinine seemed to be leveling off at 1.6. I wished it would drop a couple more points. I also got the first mention of a possible discharge by Christmas! Then, I had to sign the papers for Nathan's circumcision. Of course I journaled about that too!

> *Signed papers for circumcision. Poor baby! Mommy loves you so much!! I just hate all you've been through and are still going through. But you're so fortunate compared to a lot of the other babies in the NICU...so fortunate and I thank God every day for you and the miracles He's performed in and through you!!*

On Sunday, they took Nathan completely off the IV! On Tuesday, Dave actually got to see Nathan for the first time in about a week, wanting to be sure he was completely over the flu before coming for a visit. Nathan's weight was up an ounce, then down half an ounce. We needed to see an upward trend before they would let him come home. Since Dave was there, the nurses had us start watching the discharge videos on safety and CPR.

On December 18, after what seemed an eternity of waiting, I finally got to drive myself to the hospital! And I spent all afternoon with Nathan without feeling bad about there being someone else there waiting on me. If possible, they want me to nurse him twice a day now. I journaled to Nathan:

> *Feel so torn between you and Ashley. Sometimes it's almost unbearable. But God's always there to lift my spirits through friends, family, phone calls, and cards.*

And then to Ashley:

> *Mommy went to hospital again....had fun but mommy still feels guilty about all this running and leaving you. Don't feel like we have any quality time together.*

With an ending note for her:

> *Mommy and daddy took you to library for new books and puzzles and tapes.*

On December 19, we had the first mention of an actual date for Nathan to come home! There was a lot of talk with the nurses about his condition and what to look for, especially in regard to dehydration. Once he did come home, I would be responsible for recording his fluid intake and output (weighing diapers) and keeping track of his weight.

The next day, my visit with Nathan was interrupted by a routine hearing test that all the babies in the NICU have before being discharged. They hook up these tiny electrodes to pick up brain waves in response to sound. We got the results the following day and I journaled:

> *Got results of hearing test. No response at all in either ear at any level of sound. Mommy devastated!! Angry!! You've been through so much (and us too!) with uncertain future concerning kidneys and now you may be deaf!!! And that unanswerable question... WHY?!?! They say could be faulty test, an obstruction or fluid around ear or you could be deaf. Will retest in a month to confirm. Mommy had VERY difficult evening mentally and emotionally. I turned the rocking chair toward the wall and cried and cried as I rocked you.*

I wasn't much better once I got home. I'd just sit and sob. Ashley kept asking me, "Are you happy?"

On Sunday, I got a call that Nathan had run out of breast milk, so I skipped church to take him some. It was a good

Nathan Still a Gift of God

thing. I needed some time alone to try and come to terms with the hearing test results. It was all too much! Everything has so put my faith to the test! I eventually reached the conclusion that God's in control of the situation, and I will let Him decide whether Nathan hears or not. He will help us all accept things, whatever the outcome. It could've been his sight. I was feeling better by evening and hoping for another miracle from above. It was during this time of battling with acceptance that God used the Disney movie "Dumbo" to speak a profound truth to me as a mother. As I'm sure you know, it's a movie about a mother elephant that had a baby named Dumbo. Dumbo had exceptionally large ears and was the laughing stock of the other animals because he was different. As I was watching the movie with my daughter, I realized that no matter what, I love my baby, and NOTHING could ever change that. Regardless of his medical condition and regardless of whether he could hear or not, I love my baby. Yes, God could use even a children's movie to relay a message and bring a distraught mother some peace.

On a more spiritual note, Virgie, a long-time family friend sent us a card congratulating us on Nathan's birth. On the front of the card was a paraphrase from Isaiah 65:18: *We will be glad and rejoice forever in that which God has created.* Very simply, I (we) would be glad and rejoice in Nathan just as God had created him to be.

Nathan finally had his circumcision and of course had a very irritable night. A nice nurse walked the floor with him, for which I am so thankful, but at the same time so resentful that it wasn't me there to take care of my baby when he needed me.

On December 23, my car wouldn't start, and I had to get Dave's mom to take me to the hospital. We were all excited about Nathan coming home—maybe even today. But when

2 Our Miracle Baby

we got there, he wasn't feeling well and he went downhill fast. He developed a high fever and his heart rate was up as well. He was red all over and very irritable. He was obviously not coming home today. They began all sorts of tests to figure out what was going on—blood, urine, even a spinal tap. They had to hook him up to an IV again for fluids and antibiotics. We eventually left. Nathan had a rough night—they almost had to put him back on the ventilator. My disappointment over him not being able to come home was replaced with deep concern over the well-being of my baby. It was prayer time—not that there seemed to be a day without a need for it lately!

Dave and I visited Nathan on Christmas Eve, bringing him his first Christmas present—a puffalump (very soft, cushy, stuffed animal of a nylon type material). We got there only to find our baby boy with an IV in his hand, another one in his head and a tube down his nose to suction stomach secretions. It broke my mother's heart—again! The tests showed nothing specific, so they decided it must be a bug that was going around. But prayers were being answered once again in that his color was a little better and his fever was down. We left to go do the family Christmas with my family, then with Dave's.

Christmas morning proved to be a big deal for Ashley. She got a new kitchen set. After opening gifts, Dave stayed home with Ashley, and they played while I went over to see Nathan. He was doing much better. They had removed the IV from his head, and somehow he had managed to wiggle the tube out of his nose himself! I left him a Christian Mother Goose tape of Ashley's for them to play for him—I was counting on good results for the next hearing test! Plus, I didn't think it would hurt to have songs about Jesus played around my little boy, whether he could hear them or not.

I came over alone a couple days later and had an extra long rocking session. Nathan was eating again and gradually working his way back up to his normal feedings. I left him "Sleep Sound in Jesus" for the nurses to play for him. The songs on this tape were like thoughts and prayers from my heart for my baby boy.

Over the next couple of days, Nathan improved so much they were able to remove all the IV's except one for antibiotics. But because of having had so many IV's, his tiny veins were shot and he kept losing them. As a result, he ended up with one in his head again for the meds.

On December 30, I got to give my baby a bath for the first time! The next day—the last day of 1991—I journaled about my visit with Nathan and where I was at in general:

> *Mommy came for afternoon visit. Nursed and fed you a bottle. They took the IV out while Mommy there... boy, were you MAD! Don't blame you with tape pulling your hair and skin. Mommy has let herself get hopes up that you're coming home tomorrow. They haven't decided for sure because you just aren't putting on weight like they want you to. Mommy's just so tired of having others take care of her baby—feed, change, answer cries, etc. I'm tired of daily runs to the hospital; I'm tired of leaving Ashley all the time. I'm tired of the mental anguish and worry. I'm just plain TIRED! I love you so dearly and want you home and want some sort of normal existence again.*

He's Finally Home!

On January 1, 1992, I journaled:

Started New Year off right...YOU CAME HOME!!! Mommy called (the hospital) *to set up CPR demo for Daddy and me. I was too afraid to ask about you coming home.* (Then when we got there) *Nurse said you could go after we finished!! WOW! Was Mommy HAPPY! And Daddy too! The long-awaited day was here! I could hardly believe it!! We pulled out of hospital drive at 3:38 p.m. after much packing and carrying. First night ok...you were fine. Mommy so unorganized with a baby in house! Little over three hours sleep between feeding, pumping, and tending to you and Ashley (who isn't sleeping through the night). Have to weigh, take temperature and pulse, give medicines, fix bottles...But YOU'RE HOME! Oh! We let Ashley open your Christmas* (presents) *while you snoozed!*

January 2, was our first day at home being a real family! It was crazy having a new baby in the house again with a two-year-old, plus all the medical care Nathan required. But we were home! The other thing I did was put all the Christmas "stuff" away. We had decided to leave it all up and out until Nathan came home, but now I just wanted things to be "normal." Ashley cried for me to put it back up!

Speaking of Ashley, the first day or so went well having her new little brother home. Keep in mind, all this time she had only *heard* of a little brother. She was not allowed in the NICU because of her age. But this little brother was nevertheless totally disrupting life as she knew it! Now, this little brother was home and around and requiring quite a bit of attention. By day two, we began to see behavior changes in her. I would love to have a "journal" written by her with her own thoughts and perceptions of her life during this time! Here's what I was journaling to her as her mother:

> *VERY hard headed!! Independent! STUBBORN! (Of course, you get it honest!) Not sleeping well at nights! You usually end up in bed with Daddy. Probably adjustment to Nathan. You've been center of attention for so long. Mommy and Daddy are losing their patience a lot these days. We feel so bad!!! But we're adjusting too, not to mention TIRED!*

On Sunday, January 5, we took Nathan to church for the first time. We were still attending the little one-room church that I grew up in. Everyone was so excited about him being there and surprised to see him looking so healthy after his rough start to life and all his time in the hospital.

Monday would begin a whole new way of life for us—a life that revolved around a medically involved child. I must have been off my rocker, because I decided I could take both kids to the local hospital to have Nathan's blood work done. They were both great, and we got it done but what a task—getting all of us ready and there, having blood drawn then coming back home again!

The next day brought another first. I left both kids—yes, even Nathan—with Grandma Peggy so I could go to the dentist. Strangely enough, it was not nearly as hard as when I left Ashley for the first time.

By January 8, I thought I was going crazy! No one was getting any sleep, except for Nathan. Ashley was up at night more than Nathan. She would want to sleep with Daddy, and then Dave wouldn't get any sleep. I would be on the couch or in Ashley's bed not getting any sleep. It was an absolute zoo! Adjustment time was over! No more getting into bed with Daddy. On the flip side, Nathan was doing well. He was steadily gaining weight. I had actually become accustomed to having a little one in the house again. I certainly was not organized or getting anything done, but I was getting used to having Nathan at home and enjoying him tremendously! He was such a content baby and so-o-o-o cute! He actually smiled at me—and, no, it wasn't gas! What a joy!

By the January 11, I had cabin fever and was LONELY! I was on the job twenty-four-seven. Don't get me wrong. I loved being a mother, but I needed a break! Then it came. Grandma Peggy had us down for supper, and that same night Ashley slept all night and Nathan slept for five hours straight! Of course I didn't sleep because I kept thinking something was wrong with Nathan! Turns out my instincts were right. The next day his heart rate was up. He also had loose stools and was just not himself. I called his doctor in Charlottesville, and I had to take him in for a checkup. Seems he had a bug of some sort. His creatinine was actually down to 1.3 though! They said to keep a close eye on him. I didn't know what I'd do if he ended up in the hospital again. But whatever it was, it was short lived, and Nathan was back to himself in no time.

Of course, there was always comic relief of some sort. One evening I was enjoying a rare soak in the tub and had failed to lock the door. Ashley came in and was tugging at her "breasts" saying "my breasts too little...no get milk until they get big." Oh, the joy of being a parent! Speaking of Ashley, she had also invented an imaginary friend, Harry the Dirty Dog. He was the main character in a children's book that we had read over and over and over to her. Ashley had amazingly memorized it word for word and would recite the story as she turned the pages. "Harry" went with us everywhere, including the hospital for blood work! I was sure the invention of Harry was all a part of her surviving the chaos of our daily lives.

On Sunday, January 19, we all went to church with Grandma Peggy. Reverend Hutton mentioned that the "miracle baby" was there and what a joy it was to see him on "Sanctity of Human Life Day." I just beamed with the joy of all God had done! Well, as good as any mother could beam while her two-year-old is crying and asking, "Is it over yet?"

That Monday, we went for a visit to see Dr. Howards, the urologist. He said the kidneys still look the same, and we didn't have to come back for 6 months. Dave and I actually went out for dinner—alone! What a nice change of pace!

We fell into a daily routine of sorts. We were actually doing normal family stuff. Nathan began losing his baby hair and filling out his clothes as he gained weight. Once when he was fussy, Ashley let him suck on her fingers to quiet him down. It was so cute! Nathan's ongoing antibiotic was causing diarrhea. The doctor suggested a little bit of yogurt to offset it. What a disaster! He vomited for the next two hours! Boy, was I upset!

On Sunday, January 26, I fulfilled a promise I made to God. While I was pregnant with Nathan and we didn't know if he would live or die, I promised God that if He would heal our baby, I'd use His "miracle baby" as a witness to His awesome power. Well, God had fulfilled His end of the bargain; now, it was my turn. I shared a brief testimony at church. I was nervous, to say the least, even in front of family and friends I'd known all my life, but I did it.

By January 30, only a month into life at home with two children, I wrote in both Ashley's and Nathan's journals that I just couldn't keep up the daily entries anymore. I was just hoping to make weekly entries at this point! I also journaled about Nathan's follow-up hearing test scheduled for the next day:

> *Mommy's really nervous about your hearing test tomorrow. I had sorta put the thought out of my mind but now it's here like it or not. I've got everyone praying for you (and us) again. I just have to accept whatever God has in store for you, me, us as a family, and our future together. Easier to put on paper than into practice I assure you! You're such a GOOD*

3 He's Finally Home!

BABY! So content all the time unless you're hungry. I actually have a child who sleeps! Health wise you're doing okay. Gaining weight. You're starting to smile a lot now. Such a joy to see your face light up. Mommy thanks God every day for you and for helping us to make the decisions we made. I can't help but think what if...what if we'd taken the easy way out? What we would have missed!! And at only two months you've already had a big impact on people. You're known as the "miracle baby or as "special." Mommy just smiles with pride and joy and lots of praise to God. Like I said...I don't know what tomorrow's test may hold but whatever the findings, I love you very, very much! With or without your hearing, you're my precious baby boy and nothing can ever change that.

On February 5, we got the results of Nathan's hearing test. According to the test, Nathan was "severely to profoundly hearing impaired." It showed some response in the right ear but none in the left. They were optimistic that with a hearing aid Nathan may be able to pick up enough speech to be able to communicate orally rather than needing sign language. It certainly was not the results I was hoping for! As a mom, I was heartbroken! But I began working on getting him into a hearing impaired program for infants wanting him to have absolutely every advantage possible in dealing with his hearing loss.

We had begun visiting other churches. At the church we had been attending, Ashley was the only child of any age. She needed to be at a church with classes and activities for children. We visited Wayne Hills Baptist Church, which not only had lots of activities and opportunities for children, but also had a deaf ministry. Plus, they had plenty of things for adults as well. Our first Sunday visiting, Ashley acted up, and Dave had to take her out and spank her. Later that day, after being prompted by her father to talk to Jesus about how she had behaved in church, she bowed her head and said, "I'm sorry Jesus I was a bad girl in church." It was precious!

On February 11, I had a follow-up appointment with Dr. Ferguson who had performed the in utero surgery and delivered Nathan. I took my little miracle baby with me to show him off. Dr. Ferguson took Nathan, held him and loved on him—you could just feel the bond between the two of them! It was such a touching moment, and here I was without my camera! In talking with Dr. Ferguson, he informed me that he had only performed this procedure five times and, of the five, Nathan's was the worst case as far as any hope that it would actually work. But he said of the five, Nathan did the best of all! He also said he had attended a medical conference where he had discussed Nathan's case at length. Seems our little miracle baby had become quite popular and was even amazing the medical world!

There was a new song out called "Sometimes Miracles Hide" by Bruce Carroll, and I went out and bought the tape because it had become our theme song in a way. It's a song about a couple who were faced with the same choice we were and chose to let God work His will. It was our story! Oh, how I cried the first time I heard it! And every time since!

I had continued to pump and provide breast milk for Nathan, even after coming home from the hospital. He had such poor muscle tone even in his face that nursing was much more difficult than bottle feeding. So I thought, and the doctors agreed, if we were going to stick with the bottle, it would be okay to at least begin supplementing with formula. What a disaster! We tried formula with Nathan on Thursday, and he vomited until Saturday! It got so bad we had to take him in for blood work. They also put him on a different antibiotic just in case it was a reaction to the meds. Under the circumstances, I had no choice but to continue to pump and feed him breast milk by bottle.

3 He's Finally Home!

February 16 was Dave's birthday and the day we dedicated Nathan at my childhood church. It was a lovely service focusing on the important role of being a parent and of course making reference to what a miracle Nathan was. My brother Dave wrote a special song and sang it, and my sister Bec sang a song by Michael Card called "Wordless Ones." What a nice day!

Nathan Still a Gift of God

Our New Norm

In order to stay home with Ashley after she was born, I had begun babysitting a little boy who was a couple of months older than she. He then had a baby sister, and I had been keeping both of them up until the last couple of months of my pregnancy with Nathan. They both were finally able to return. They were about the ages of mine which made life at the Sours' household interesting, to say the least, especially with all of Nathan's medical demands. But it was only a few days a week, and we certainly could use any extra income we could get. The only problem was that we never knew what Nathan was going to do, medically speaking. On February 24, I had the kids, and Nathan began vomiting and running a fever. I ended up having to call the children's grandmother to come from about forty-five minutes away to pick them up so I could take Nathan in to see the doctor. They took blood and urine, which just broke my heart. (If you remember, Nathan still has the vesicostomy they had placed at birth, and getting a sterile urine sample from an opening below your belly button can prove quite challenging at times.) I was a basket case with worry.

Two days later it was back to the doctor again. Nathan was put on yet another antibiotic for infection. Two days after that, we were back AGAIN drawing more blood and taking more urine. This time Grandma Peggy came and watched Ashley and the kids so I could take Nathan to the doctor. (I eventually gave up the babysitting because it was too much for me and not fair to them or their parents.) The local doctor thought it best for Nathan's doctors in Charlottesville to take a look at him. Once at U.Va., they had to do another set of blood and urine tests. Nathan screamed. I cried. I had had enough worry and pain for one week and I knew Nathan felt the same. My poor little baby!

They ended up admitting Nathan to the hospital. Even though I expected it, I still cried. But I certainly wasn't ready to hear it would be for seven to ten days! They gave him liquid Tylenol for the fever, but as soon as it touched his mouth, he vomited. (Ashley had been the same way. She could never take Tylenol by mouth without vomiting. And just like her, Nathan would have to go with suppositories.) Once they got us into a room, they took him across the hall to an exam room where they were going to do a spinal tap and start an IV. It took them about an hour. Nathan's veins were not only tiny but, by this point, were used up from all the sticks and IVs since he was born. It was difficult finding a good vein. Boy, did he scream as they worked on him! And there wasn't a thing I could do about it except sit across the hall in his room with the lights out and listen to my baby scream. I sobbed and prayed it would soon be over! What a horrible hour! A terribly long hour! Dave got there the last few minutes of the whole ordeal, and I just sobbed on his shoulder until they finally brought Nathan out to me. I just held him and kissed him and cried some more. He was exhausted! And very fretful. Oh, how I hated leaving him in the hospital alone! But I had a little girl at home who needed me too, and she could understand much better "mommy's gone." What an awful week it had been!

    Dave, Ashley and I all went over the next morning to see Nathan. He had a room all to himself so that made it nicer, especially with a two-year-old. Dave finally left to take Ashley home, but I stayed all day. Nathan was hoarse from all the screaming and crying from the night before. He was pitiful to look at. He had an IV in his head after the one in his hand failed during the night. Over the course of his ten-day-stay, he would go through a total of four IVs—one in his hand, two in his head, and one in his foot. I would go over every day and visit and take milk. As he began to feel better, I was making two trips over a day to keep up with his appetite! With everything going on, my milk supply was sluggish to say the least.

    During Nathan's stay in the hospital, I had an opportunity

4 Our New Norm

to meet another mom whose son had a very similar blockage, only they didn't discover his until after he was born. He had worse kidney damage but a better creatinine level. It was just nice to have someone to talk to who had "been there, done that" sort of thing. Nathan finally came home and boy was it good to have him back! He was on yet another new antibiotic. Hopefully this one would work!

Nathan had another hearing test on March 17. He had the brain wave testing as well as some testing in a sound booth. It showed maybe a little improvement in the right ear. He still couldn't get his hearing aids—seems his paperwork had been misplaced. But the good news is the $1,000 or so price tag would be covered under Children's Specialty Services. As if life isn't crazy enough, the hearing test showed a brain wave pattern consistent with fluid on the brain. They contacted Dr. Castello, Nathan's local pediatrician, and set up a CAT scan for the very next morning. I guess I was getting tough, because I didn't overreact like I typically did. The scan showed if there was any fluid on the brain, it was not enough to worry about for now. We'd just have to wait and see.

On Thursday, March 19, Nathan was vomiting. By Sunday, he had discolored urine and pus coming from his vesicostomy. I had trouble communicating the urgency of the situation with our local hospital on a weekend, so Dave and I said, "forget it" and made the trip over the mountain to U.Va. where they knew Nathan. It was Dave's first time to see for himself what we go through in the emergency room with drawing blood and starting IVs. (He usually stayed home with Ashley while I took Nathan.) Poor thing! He sat in the corner with tears in his eyes as Nathan screamed at the top of his lungs while they attempted to start an IV and do blood work. Again, I guess I was just getting tough or maybe calloused. I just looked on as they worked. They admitted Nathan and he would spend fourteen days in the hospital this time.

I was making the daily trips as usual to the hospital to see Nathan and deliver milk. On one particular morning I arrived on the seventh floor only to hear my baby crying—a mother just knows her baby's cry. He wasn't in his room. I scouted around until I found him in an exam room being stuck for the fifth or sixth time in an attempt to find a vein for an IV. This would be his third IV already. Oh, how I hurt for my baby! So much to go through for such a little guy! With this hospital stay, I found myself coming over in the mornings and staying most of the day and then returning home to Ashley in the evenings. I felt like there was just too much to keep on top of if I wasn't there. Being on a regular pediatric floor, he just didn't get the one-on-one attention that he did in the NICU. And even as wonderful as the nurses were, I was his mother and nobody is there for you like your mommy!

On March 26, Nathan had a renal scan. They injected him with radioactive dye and strapped him to a table for 90 minutes while they watched the dye travel through his urinary system. Thank goodness I was there and that Nathan was such a good baby. With a binky (pacifier), his fascination with the cross stitch pattern on my shirt, a little napping, and the Lord's help, we got through it. After reviewing the results of the scan, they decided to do another test at the beginning of the next week called a Whittaker Test. In this test, they would take a needle and insert it into Nathan's bad kidney to test for pressure. Then, they would flush fluid through to give some indication of any blockages. Should another infection occur, the physicians were tentatively planning to go ahead and remove the blockage and repair the vesicostomy. I had always thought they were waiting because Nathan was so small, but it was also because they were concerned about the possible pressure on the kidneys once the bladder was closed. Too much pressure could cause further damage.

On a more personal note regarding Nathan, a mother can

always find joy in her baby. Nathan was about four months old as I wrote in his journal:

> You're a very social baby always smiling and talking! You're starting to reach for things, occasionally grabbing them. You're slowly gaining weight and growing. You have rolls of fat on wrists and hands, legs, and have at least three chins!!! Ha ha! Had picture taken at Roses a few weeks ago and the girl asked to keep your picture to use in her portfolio for advertising. Mommy so proud!! Everyone calls you a "Gerber baby" cuz you're so cute!!! Of course mommy agrees 100 percent!! Oh, I love you so much and hope this is the last we see of the hospital for awhile although I am managing a little better this time. It's amazing what you can get accustomed to and survive—with God's help of course. All the nurses and your roomies tell Mommy what a good baby you are. How beautiful you are...even say you have "angelic" features! One of the renal doctors is calling you "Nate." And your Aunt Tammy shared that you and your circumstances have had a big impact on her spiritually. At least some good is coming of all this. I know it sure has had positive effects on Mommy and Daddy and our faith! I hope one day you can appreciate your witness to people even at a young age.

On April 2nd, while still in the midst of Nathan's hospital stay, I journaled:

> Things have been so hectic running back and forth to the hospital trying to at least do laundry at home so I have "drawers" to wear and seeing after Ashley as best as I can...Whew! Am I tired! Mommy had an emotional breakdown Monday. I held up as long as I could and then I just had to let it out. Grandma Peggy was there for me as usual. She's such a special person to me especially since my mommy died. But I'm better

now.

I eventually lost track of all the IVs Nathan had and lost during this hospital stay. His head seemed to be a popular spot of late. He had needle pricks all over his arms, hands, feet, and head where IVs had been not to mention more than one patch of missing hair, and even skin, where the tape had left its mark. The last few days of his stay, they finally gave up with the IV and gave him his last couple doses of antibiotic by injection rather than start yet another IV. Then to top everything off, they had to put Nathan in isolation because he and Ashley had been exposed to chicken pox. I had been spending most of the day there anyway but now with him in isolation, I felt even more compelled to be there, especially after I came in one morning to find him screaming at the top of his lungs and it was obvious he had been for some time. I was so mad—isolation or not! As a result, I began spending twelve or more hours a day at the hospital with Nathan, playing with him and tending to him. I already mentioned getting less individual attention, but in isolation it was even worse since every time anyone entered his room, he or she had to put on a gown and gloves.

We had been trying all week to have this Whittaker Test done. It was scheduled for Tuesday, and Dave and I both came over around 8 a.m. Nathan hadn't eaten since before midnight and was not a happy camper to say the least! We took turns rocking, standing, and bouncing with him until finally at 3 p.m. they reported they had a scheduling problem and wouldn't be able to do the test after all! Boy, were we upset! Sixteen hours or so without anything to eat or drink! Nathan downed about nine ounces once we started feeding him. Dave couldn't thaw the breast milk out fast enough! All three of us were exhausted.

The test was rescheduled for Wednesday at 1 p.m. Guess what? It didn't happen again! Of course this time Nathan only went for four or five hours without food but it was still an exhausting morning. Then it was scheduled for the third day in a row and this time for 8 a.m. I got there at 5:30 a.m. just because I thought he'd be fussy—he was fast asleep! The test took about three hours. Well maybe I should say the *attempt* at the test took about three hours. They did manage to get the needle in to inject the dye into the kidney. But after twelve needle sticks into Nathan's little back, they were unable to get even one needle in to check for the pressure in the kidney. They finally gave up. By then, the dye had begun to work its way through the bladder and out the vesicostomy indicating that if there was any blockage, it was minimal at best. Nathan was in an amazingly good mood in spite of what he had just been through!

Nathan finally came home from this latest hospital stay on Sunday, April 5, just in time to make it to church. What a joy and what a relief! We left with a new creatinine level of 1.0!!! I was really hopeful that if we could just get through his first year, avoid any more infections and get his surgery done, Nathan would do great! God had just worked too many miracles in and through him to stop now!

Now that we were home, I was trying to get organized and cleaned up plus muddle through all the insurance stuff. What a mess! There was no way we could pay what they wanted, when they wanted it! And trying to keep track of all the appointments, the house, Dave, Ashley, Nathan—I was on overload! Then after being home for barely five days, I was in a panic and off to the doctor again because Nathan had developed a fever and was vomiting. It turned out to be a false alarm, thank goodness. I just didn't think I could do another hospital stay, especially so soon after the challenges of the last one. With the Lord's help, I was hoping to see some light at the end of a very long tunnel.

Our reprieve from infection didn't last long. By April 24, Nathan had yet another infection. This time, however, we were able to have a nurse from Home IV come once a day and give Nathan an injection. Though not pleasant, it was

Nathan Still a Gift of God

so much better than spending endless days in the hospital and battling IVs. After so many days of it, Nathan didn't even cry after the injection. But just in case he did, Ashley would crawl under the bed when the nurse was about to give Nathan the injection because she didn't want to see him cry. Even though they had said if he got another infection they would do the surgery, they decided to wait a little while longer because of his size and age.

Despite a crazy, often unpredictable life, we really did try to be as "normal" as possible. Dave and Ashley went with Rusty, Tammy, Ben, and Annie (Dave's brother and his family) to the circus. Because of Nathan's infection, we thought it best if I stayed home with him. When they got home the first thing Ashley said was, "They shot a man out of a cannon!" That must have made quite an impression on her because that was what she talked about the most. She also said there were lots of clowns, "elfanants" (elephants) that danced, a motorcycle on the high wire, a white tiger, and horses. Dave said she stood on the chair beside him with her arm around him and didn't move the entire first half! I was so sad I missed her first circus! I could've cried!

We all went to a local zoo with Rusty's family. Of course, Nathan was too young to enjoy it, although he was good. Ashley, on the other hand, had a ball! According to Ashley and her cousin Ben, they saw "mamas" (llamas), "honkeys" (donkeys), "magillas" (gorillas) and of course more "elfanants". Dave had a good time too until one of the "mamas" spit in his face! Even then, it was still a nice day.

A personal note in Ashley's journal:

> *You're growing up so fast!! TOO fast!! You're learning new things all the time. It's fun watching you grow and teaching you new things but I'm gonna miss my baby Ashley!!! Oh! The other day you gave mommy money for using potty.* (We had been using a little incentive for her to use the potty.) *Cracked me up!! You're starting to sing right much now but you get*

4 Our New Norm

> *embarrassed if you think someone's watching. The other day you sang and danced to the Old Macdonald farm tape. A riot!!! And today you must have learned "If You're Happy and You Know It" at Sunday school cuz you've been singing and clapping it. Yesterday, you wrote your name (or copied it) for the first time!! What a bright child! You're interested in helping me cook now too. You like mixing pancakes, muffins... you even break eggs now and spoon muffins into pan. Like to stir tea and juice too. Speaking of food...you love to eat BUTTER!! What a character!! But we love you!!!*

And then in Nathan's journal:

> *You're eating rice cereal. You're not too impressed with it by any means. Started carrots. Really like 'em! And you're starting to get hang of this spoon deal. You're a real "conversationalist" now. Love it when someone talks to you face to face. Seem to hear "hi" and "baby" in deep voices. You lost all your hair in the hospital—just a little fuzz now. You're "playing with things"—reaching...grabbing...like to swing.... You're growing up so fast. You're giggling...even when I change your clothes or just making noises at you. Which brings me to your hearing. We haven't gotten your aids yet. Supposed to be fitted in couple weeks. I think you're hearing quite a bit. Just last week I was talking to you and you turned to my voice. I was so excited!! You can just see the hint of your bottom two teeth. Trying so hard to roll over but haven't quite succeeded yet. Ashley really is doing so well with you and your many doctor visits. If she doesn't see you she'll ask where you're at and when I come back from doctor she'll ask "Where's Nathan?" I think she still remembers all the times in the hospital.*

Now it's back to reality, at least our reality. The day following our trip to the zoo was Sunday, and after church,

Nathan Still a Gift of God

Nathan was showing signs of an infection again. So it was off to the local emergency room for the afternoon. While we were there, Nathan passed a mucous plug from his penis, and then he peed! Keep in mind that because of the blockage and, of course, the vesicostomy, Nathan had never peed "naturally!" It was quite the pleasant surprise! We were promptly sent to U.Va., where we ended up staying for a week. I stayed in the hospital with Nathan this time. But after a while, I had "Ashley-itis" and was crying at the hospital because I missed her so much. One night, I decided to go home and see my baby girl. The nurses said they had trouble getting Nathan to eat and sleep that night. Of course, I wanted to think it was because he was rotten for his mommy! Talk about being torn in two! I kept wondering if we would ever have a normal life again.

They decided to do an IV this time so he wouldn't get immune to the injections. It lasted less than twenty-four hours. So it was back to injections. We had horrible experiences with blood drawings as usual and even the injections this time. Nathan had something called a cystoscopy where they inserted a scope through his penis and examined their way up into his bladder. They discovered the blockage was all but gone with just a sliver left—another miracle in my book! And his bladder wall was not as thickened as they had anticipated. This was encouraging news for when they would relocate the ureter on the bladder—yet another part of this impending surgery we would have one day. But they could find nothing that could be causing his recurring infections. We finally came home and continued the injections. Nathan's little legs and hips were so knotty and bruised from all the injections; it was pitiful!

On Tuesday, we were informed we would have surgery on June 4, closing the vesicostomy, relocating the ureter and removing any remaining blockage. Then on Friday, we found out that we will NOT be doing surgery after all. They had decided to try "flushing" Nathan's bladder out one or

4 Our New Norm

two times a day with an antibiotic solution of some sort. It was very frustrating changing mental gears but we kept putting it all in God's hands as to what was best for Nathan. We sure didn't know!

In the middle of all the medical chaos, Dave and I tried to spend time with Ashley. We got her a Mickey Mouse fishing pole and took her fishing at a local pond. She caught three perch and one crappie with her pole using worms. Dave, using his hi-tech fishing paraphernalia, caught nothing! We also took her to a local carnival. She had a blast! She rode everything including the ferris wheel and enjoyed a snow cone and popcorn. What a fun evening we had!

Then once again, it was back to reality. On Monday, June 1, I had to get "trained" on how to flush Nathan's bladder. The most difficult part was getting Nathan to lay still. I had to fill a very large syringe with the antibiotic solution and insert the broad tip into the opening of the vesicostomy far enough to insure the fluid would get into the bladder and then "squirt" it in there. (That's my technical medical term.) We started the flushing that Friday.

Then, Ashley got sick. She started out with a cold that simply wouldn't go away. Eventually, I took her to see the doctor, and they did a strep test. Then, she started vomiting and had diarrhea for a week. I decided to take her back to the doctor just to be on the safe side, and this time he wanted to do blood work. I was used to doctors and blood work with Nathan but not with Ashley. She cried a little but otherwise did fine. I think the whole ordeal bothered me more than it did her. Whatever it was, it eventually ran its course, and she was back to normal.

Whatever bug Ashley had, she passed it on to Nathan, and we ended up spending three nights in the hospital. Thinking he was better, I dared to take Ashley to Vacation Bible School a couple days later—I actually thought I could help teach a class. Nathan threw up on a nursery worker, and it was back to the doctor. But things turned around, and we actually finished the week of Bible School. We had survived yet another hectic couple of weeks.

On June 22, Nathan FINALLY got his hearing aids. He did okay with them at first, although we couldn't tell an obvious difference in his hearing with them on. Then, they became chew toys! He'd just slip his little finger up to his ear, grab hold, pull them out and promptly put them in his mouth. I hate to use the word again, but how frustrating! However, when he had his next hearing test, they turned them up and he did thirty points (or decibels) better than before! I was so excited! Diane, his infant coordinator, reminded me that didn't necessarily mean the comprehension was there, which sort of burst my bubble. Nevertheless, it was indeed good news.

Dave and I started weekly sign language classes in Charlottesville in July. We learned the ABCs and a few basic words. I could read sign ok, but my fingers didn't prove to be very coordinated. Dave was just the opposite. He did better signing than reading. I guess together we made a pretty good team.

Call it insanity, but we decided to borrow Dave's brother's camper and take a weekend camping trip with some friends of ours. We left in the pouring down rain and Nathan screamed the entire way. It continued to rain Saturday morning, but the weather finally broke so Dave and Ashley actually managed to have fun in the pool Saturday afternoon. But that evening as I was flushing Nathan's bladder (no vacation from medical stuff), I heard Ashley scream. As I turned to see what was happening with her, Nathan slipped off the bed and rolled into the floor. He absolutely screamed bloody murder for what seemed like forever! Nathan apparently hit his mouth as he fell, making it difficult for him to suck a bottle for a few days. We packed up that night and came home, vowing it would be a long time before we tried that again.

Ashley had two front teeth that were darkened on the

4 Our New Norm

ends, and we set up an appointment to have a pediatric dentist take a look at them. What a riot! It took me, the nurse, and the dentist to hold her down so he could manage to pry open her mouth just to get a peek at them! He said they were okay for now, but what an experience! Never a dull moment with the Sours!

In addition to everything else, it seemed Nathan also had some developmental delays. He was late with pretty much all of the milestones of an infant—lifting his head and rolling over for instance. In order to address his delays, we started going to physical therapy once a week to strengthen his upper body. There was also a concern that he wasn't gaining weight as he should, and so we would need to be looking at his diet and ways to beef him up. One of the main ways was adding this liquid fat to his foods as much as possible. Could our lives possibly get any more interesting?!

Ashley's third birthday rolled around, and it was cause for lots of reminiscing about both of my babies. With Ashley, it was just hard to believe my baby girl was three! With Nathan, it was hard to believe how much had happened since that fateful day of being told our baby had a life-threatening urinary blockage.

Nathan's journal:

> *And this time last year your adventure and fight for life began. It seems like another lifetime in a way. Boy, how far we've come!!!! The miracles in your short life!!! The people you have astounded and amazed with your struggles and progress.*

Ashley's journal:

> *This time last year our lives were in total turmoil. But look at Nathan now! MIRACLE!!!! Mommy and Daddy love you two so much!! We are trying so hard to be good parents. Some days it's so hard to do what's right. Parenting is such an important job and we don't*

want to mess up. Hopefully one day you'll look back and think we did "okay" at least. Anyway, no matter how we're doing—we love you very much!

Making Some Progress

As I said earlier, we had been visiting other churches to find one that best suited the needs of our family. We eventually decided on Wayne Hills Baptist Church. On August 16, exactly one year to the day of Nathan's in utero surgery, Dave and I were both re-baptized, making public our faith in Christ and becoming official members of WHBC. Dave had been baptized around the age of fourteen not really having a clue what it was all about. He marks my mom's death as the catalyst for him seeking and finding his personal salvation in Jesus Christ.

I, on the other hand, went forward at a southern gospel concert around the age of fourteen with the full realization that I was a sinner in need of a Savior. Sadly, that's as far as it went. Now as I look back, I believe all I had was "hell insurance" at best. However, I do believe God pursued me in the years that followed, especially after Mom's death. It was during those years that my relationship with Him began to develop even though I didn't realize what was happening at the time. It wasn't until spending time at Wayne Hills and in particular with Miss Maggie, the church's prayer warrior, that I truly came to understand what having a personal relationship with Him and making Him Lord of my life was all about. Miss Maggie took me under her wing and became a "spiritual mother" to me. Growing up in a rather legalistic environment, it was very difficult for me to understand "grace." So Miss Maggie did what she does best. She got out the flannel graph that she used with the children to explain God's grace, helping me to understand the gift of salvation and a personal relationship with God. She said that everyone, including myself, had sinned. She illustrated this with a female figure representing myself and placed a splotch of black on her to represent my sin. She explained that this sin separated me from God, however, God loved me so much that He was not willing to let me live apart from Him but there had to be a payment for my sin. So God sent His only Son Jesus who lived the perfect life that I never could and was willing to die on the cross in my place to pay the price for my sin. She then took my "black sin" that was on the woman figure that represented me and placed it on the figure of Jesus as He died on the cross. Somewhere in that transferring of the "black sin" from me to Jesus, it clicked with me! He took my sin on Himself and paid the price so I did not have to! I got it! She then went on to explain that He died and was buried but that He came back to life again on the third day and is now in Heaven and, if I will accept what He did for me on the cross, I can go to Heaven when I die and live with Him forever. She then guided me in a prayer accepting this gift and this time I prayed with a new understanding of what God had done for me. All through the wonderful medium of flannel graph! Then as I said earlier, on August 16, Dave and I both decided to put down a spiritual marker so to speak and be baptized, this time knowing full well what we were doing and what it all meant.

The remainder of August and into the month of September was filled with visits to physical therapy, hearing tests, sign classes and a whole host of other appointments. On top of that, I was canning and freezing as much as I could in addition to crafting to help make ends meet. I was busy to say the least! Nathan had been vomiting quite a bit. I think it was because I was a bit over zealous with his fat additive, because when I cut back on it, the vomiting stopped. He still wasn't gaining weight overall. I was at my wits' end counting calories and grams of protein, adding fats and trying to keep some kind of record of it all. I decided to do what I could, but just leave the rest to God because I certainly couldn't make him gain weight. We also had another scare concerning fluid on his brain. An ultrasound showed no change from the last time, although this time the procedure absolutely infuriated Nathan.

5 Making Some Progress

I made a brief notation in both Ashley's and Nathan's journals:

> (Ashley) *You're starting to look more like a little girl and less like a baby. You're sharp as a tack!! And stubborn as a mule!! But overall a blessing from above.*
>
> (Nathan) *Everyone still adores you. And you're really a good baby except for being ROTTEN, but I wouldn't have it any other way!*

It was October. Nathan was still fighting vomiting, while I was fighting tears of frustration—both of us battling rather unsuccessfully. Dr. Castello said enough is enough and was going to try and get to the bottom of it. An upper GI test revealed reflux and, with medication, Nathan's problem with vomiting greatly improved. Then, he got another bug that had him so dehydrated he almost ended up in the hospital. We simply could not win! But even with the bug, Nathan managed to hit an all-time high of fourteen pounds and five ounces! Still not what an almost one-year-old child should weigh by any means, but at least we were heading in the right direction for a change.

His physical therapy was paying off too. As a result, he now had much better head control and upper body strength. Nathan could actually get up on his knees and elbows and manage to pull himself along the floor. Diane, our infant coordinator, started a sign language class in our home for some of our family members. Now, Dave and I wouldn't have to make the trip to Charlottesville each week. And on a fun note, for Halloween Ashley was a bunny, Nathan was a little girl dressed in his sister's ruffled-bottom pajamas complimented by a bonnet with bows while Dave and I were clowns.

November and December were filled with appointments of all sorts. One big milestone for me was that I was finally able to quit pumping breast milk. For eleven months—yes, eleven months—I had faithfully pumped so Nathan could have the benefit of his mother's milk. We were never able to get anywhere with him actually nursing. To give you an idea of how bad it actually was, I would experience "letdown" whenever I turned the breast pump on! Yes, it was past time to return the dreaded machine!

Another milestone for Nathan was that he wore shoes for the first time. Not really necessary at this point but Ashley really liked him in shoes. (Years later, at twenty-one, she still has a shoe fetish!) We also celebrated Nathan's first birthday with a party in the fellowship hall at Grandma Peggy's church. We probably went overboard, but we were celebrating much more than our baby turning one year old. There were lots of people, even more kids. It was loud and wild and I'm glad he would only have one first birthday, but it was a wonderful day! And by his one year checkup, Nathan weighed a whopping fifteen pounds!

Now that he was a year old, I decided to start experimenting with feeding Nathan different kinds of food. I took a chance and gave him French fries in tiny pieces. He didn't vomit and absolutely loved them! Then I tried Cheerios. Then bread and ice cream from a food bar. All of a sudden this eating thing hit him. Whether it was the new foods or the fascination that he could do it himself, he loved it!

With Christmas around the corner, I took Nathan to see a signing Santa. Let's just say if our Christmas depended on my signing, we'd all be in trouble! Nathan was fascinated with his beard. The holidays were a busy time of course, but the real kicker came when Ashley got up on Christmas with a strange "pimple." Through the course of all our family activities the single pimple turned into multiple "pimples." It seems Ashley had come down with chicken pox and exposed the entire family, including her uncle Steven, who had never had chicken pox as a child. About a week later,

5 Making Some Progress

Nathan developed chicken pox along with his uncle and his two cousins.

Nathan, of course, could not do anything the easy way. One morning he woke up with chicken pox, and that very evening I discovered a bulge the size of an egg in his tiny groin. I called the doctor. Turns out it was a hernia. They decided to go ahead and take care of the hernia and the closing of the vesicostomy all at the same time. Surgery was scheduled for March 4. I didn't know if I could wait that long. They didn't particularly like him being on the flush long-term and now with a hernia that could strangulate — well, it was just all too much.

With that hanging over our heads, Nathan also had an appointment with the eye clinic. Nathan had a problem with his eyes "floating" or crossing which would require surgery to correct. The appointment was a horrible experience! Let's just say Nathan didn't exactly hit it off with the doctor! The doctor gave us a cream for Nathan's eyes to use for a week. Then he would recheck the next week, with surgery scheduled in two weeks. The surgery itself went okay, but Nathan wasn't allowed to eat or drink until we got him home. Boy, was he ever mad!

Nathan Still a Gift of God

Victories and Challenges

January proved to be quite the month of milestones for Nathan. He was growing and developing by leaps and bounds. He was sitting up fairly well. He was standing up against things and starting to get the idea of hanging on and "cruising" around them. He was pulling up to a stand. He could squirm across the floor on his elbows and boy, could he move in his walker! And was he ever a mama's boy!

They moved the vesicostomy surgery and hernia repair up to February 18. I was nervous to say the least. Nathan got another bug with vomiting. I decided to keep him in until the surgery. I just couldn't risk him catching anything else. Nathan's renal doctors were very concerned about his lack of weight gain. But was it any wonder with all the bugs he would catch! And he wasn't sleeping well since having the chickenpox which of course meant neither was I. I spent much of most nights walking and rocking him. I was sure it would be nothing compared to what we were in for in a couple of weeks!

February 18 came all too quickly. I had a very difficult time getting mentally and emotionally ready for this surgery. I had a very gloomy outlook. Finally, with prayer and encouragement from Miss Maggie, I found that wonderful peace and strength I needed to face the day. Surgery was scheduled for 7:30 a.m., but we had to be there by 6:30 a.m. There was a little delay in actually starting—as usual. It was a long procedure—5 ½ to 6 hours. The first epidural didn't take, so they had to do a second. They removed a good bit of the ureters then re-implanted them both on the bladder, which was an extra bonus because they didn't think it would be possible. Then they closed the vesicostomy and fixed the hernia, which Dr. Howards said was "very large for such a little boy!" Dr. Howards seemed pleased with the surgery. We had lots of visitors during the procedure. Grandma Peggy was there all day. It was nice to have a support group at times like these.

Nathan had a horrible night following surgery, sleeping very little. Of course I got no sleep and was exhausted. They added some medicine to the epidural, and it seemed to help. I lost all track of time being in the hospital. Nathan did well but had problems with pain and discomfort. He got morphine, opium, Tylenol, Benedryl plus narcotics through the epidural! We had a couple of setbacks along the way as well. They put him on an oral antibiotic in the same family as the one he reacted to once before, thinking it was different enough and would be okay. Well, it wasn't, and Nathan spent the weekend vomiting. They clamped his "supra pubic tube" on Thursday 25 to see if he could pee on his own. He didn't; he just leaked urine around the site of the tube in his bladder. His creatinine skyrocketed to 2.6 or 2.9—I can't remember which.

In the midst of everything going on from the surgery and all the urinary issues, they decided to start n-g feeds (naso-gastro) to get some weight on him. This is where they insert a tube into his nose and thread it into his tummy, hook the tube to a machine and pump milk through the tube at a constant rate. That was a nightmare in and of itself! They of course had to adjust the rates—trying to figure out how much milk to pump in a given length of time. They went too fast, and he vomited. They switched to a milk-based formula, and he vomited. Between the surgery, the slow recovery, being groggy from the pain medication and now playing around with the right formula, Nathan was losing weight daily to the point that his skin was saggy. He looked absolutely pitiful.

I had about all I could take and decided to go home for the night. Dave's mom and cousin Mary Jane came and spent the night with Nathan so I could leave and be home with Dave and Ashley, take a shower and hopefully get some much needed sleep. It was a nice little break, which only made it harder to go back to the hospital. Nathan was terrified of being touched now. He was leery of people in general, which was so not like him. I couldn't get out of his sight now, or he'd literally freak out. This was by far the most difficult hospital stay yet!

They tried clamping the tube again after a couple of days. Nathan peed a little, but urine was still mainly leaking from around the tube in his tummy. They did something called a cystogram where they put dye in through the supra pubic tube and took x-rays as it traveled through his system. The test showed nothing that would explain Nathan not being able to pee on his own. They thought maybe the pressure in the bladder was too high for it to function properly, and they began talking about doing a vesicostomy again!

On March 1, God gave me a word that spoke directly into our circumstances and to the need to be patient and wait on Him in the midst: Psalm 37:34 *Wait on the Lord and keep His way and He shall exalt you to inherit the land; when the wicked are cut off, you shall see it.*

Nathan decided to take matters into his own hands and he managed to pull the supra pubic tube out on his own—it had been in so long it was almost out anyway and he just decided to help it along. The urine was still just leaking around the other tube, no peeing. They decided on a foley catheter with a bag in order to let the bladder heal more fully, and then at some point, give him another try at peeing on his own. He would most likely be able to go home once the catheter was in place.

We had lots of visitors through the course of our long fifteen-day hospital stay. Our Pastor Dan Gregg was one of the most faithful, bringing me several lunches and suppers, always with a DR Pepper! My sister Bec made it her job to be our comic relief and was such a blessing during some very difficult times. During our hospital stay, Dave and Ashley of course were regular visitors. On one particular visit, Ashley came carrying a brown paper bag tied shut with a piece of yarn. It seems Dave had had the hiccups and used a bag to breathe into. When his hiccups were gone, she thought they were in the bag, so she held it really tight until Grandma Peggy could tie it shut so no one else could get them. She brought it to me as a gift with strict instructions not to untie it. Precious! And yet a sore reminder of what I was missing out on while in the hospital and away from home and family.

Nathan did indeed come home with a catheter and a bag that we had to carefully tuck in his diaper. We also had to empty it regularly. Ashley was my little helper in that endeavor. She would hold a container while I would drain the bag into it and then she would dump the contents into the potty. It was a week until they removed the catheter. But when they did, HE PEED! A lot of prayers went up for Nathan and once again, God came through!

Nathan also came home on the tube feedings. We were to hook him up to a pump and run the feedings at night while he slept. They were going better than I expected, but I sure wouldn't miss them when they were done. For the most part, Nathan didn't seem to mind the tube in his nose, especially once they decided to use a smaller sized tube. I had to change the tube once a week, or sooner if it came out for any reason. The main reason we had to reinsert tubes more often was that if it weren't taped securely or completely to his cheek, Nathan would manage to hook his little finger under it and flip it out. It was really a bit scary, especially at night, because if he didn't pull it completely out, it could get lodged and leak fluid into his lungs and cause pneumonia or he could even choke on it. Another problem we ran into was that if it did come out at night, the pump just kept running, and we would have the sticky formula everywhere. We also learned that he needed to be elevated to help with digestion. This, too, we learned the hard way with a number of vomiting episodes. Needless to say, neither one of us was sleeping at nights.

Despite all of that, the hardest part was changing tubes. I'd first have to remove the old one, which meant removing LOTS of tape from very sensitive, delicate facial skin that would often come off with the tape. We would switch sides of his face to allow healing, but both of his little cheeks were very tender and raw. Then I'd have to lay him flat and clamp him between my knees to hold him perfectly still while I threaded the tube into his nose, down his throat and into his stomach. I'd then have to hold the tube and inject a syringe of "air" into it as I listened to his tummy with a stethoscope. If I could hear air bubbles in his tummy, that meant I had properly inserted the tube. If I didn't hear the gurgling noises, I'd have to try again. Once I was sure I had it in properly, I then had to carefully tape the tube to his face. I got better with time and practice of course but each time was an experience.

I was exhausted, grumpy, had no patience, and was having to apologize to Ashley frequently for my moods, actions, and words. She was such a little trooper through all of this. Adjusting as best as a three-year-old could to all this strange paraphernalia. Oh, to read her thoughts as she watched me "sit" on Nathan and put tubes down his nose as he squirmed and screamed. I felt so guilty about the time, extra care, and attention Nathan needed. It seemed like I was having to slight both Ashley and Dave all too often. I just hoped and prayed all of this didn't have a lasting, negative effect on her. And as if there weren't enough pressure on me already, I decided to add some more myself by reading this book about being the ideal godly wife, mother, and woman. It was a very good book, but perhaps the timing could have been a bit better!

Now that the vesicostomy was gone and his belly was all healed up, Nathan got to experience his first tub bath on Friday, March 19. (Having a vesicostomy meant we could not sit Nathan in water for fear it would flush germs and bacteria into his bladder. Up to this point, we had only been doing sponge baths.) He was a little leery at first and would only stand in the water, but once I finally got him to sit down, he seemed to sort of like it. He played with the bath toys and with Ashley, who was in the tub with him to help make him feel more at ease. But then he seemed to become aware of the fact that he was in a strange situation and wanted out. It was a start. In time, he grew to love bath time, and I had trouble getting him out!

By the end of March, Nathan, almost sixteen months old, hit a whopping sixteen pounds! He was also saying a few words: "ma-ma," "da-da," "aaa" (Ashley), "daw" (dog), repeated the "k" sound for kitty and was signing quite a bit as well. We, too, had been continuing to learn sign language. As a "test" to see how well our family members were doing, we were invited to a silent supper where, as the name implies, you are not allowed to use your voice, only sign. Toward the end of the dinner, Diane, our instructor signed to me and asked me what I had learned by being there. What I meant to sign in response to her question was that "I had learned I needed to work harder on my signing." To which everyone around me burst into laughter. I thought "how rude" since I didn't think I was doing that bad with only a few months of learning. But when Diane could stop laughing, she leaned over and informed me that what I had just signed to everyone sitting around me was "I had learned I needed to make out more!" I guess I wasn't as advanced as I thought!

On June 15, Nathan sat up on his own, and by mid-August he took his first solo steps! This was later than most children, but nevertheless they were huge milestones for Nathan, especially given his developmental delays and poor muscle tone. He was cruising around things, crawling everywhere, and into everything! I don't think even I realized how advanced he was becoming in his mobility until over the Fourth of July weekend.

That weekend Nathan was in his "Flintstone" car (the red and yellow Little Tykes car that is foot powered) and was sitting in the middle of the living room floor. I had been folding laundry and, seeing that he was content, I picked up a stack of clothes to deliver them to their destination in the bedroom. I had hardly set them down when I heard a terrible scream coming from the living room. It seems Nathan had given himself a boost and rolled the car to the bottom of the steps. He then decided to get out of his car and, in the process, somehow managed to hit his head on the bottom step. By the time I got to him, there was already a goose egg on his head. I called the ER and they of course said we needed to bring him in. They x-rayed his head but didn't find anything seriously wrong—thank goodness! But then they asked me to undress him, and they examined him and began asking me all sorts of questions. They suspected me of hitting him, especially because by the time we got to the ER, not only did he have a goose egg on his head, but apparently his face had slid across the carpet, and he had gotten rug burn as well down the side of his face. Once I undressed him, the questions only continued because Nathan was still a scrawny little thing with lots of bruises all over from all the needle sticks for blood and IVs and from all the injections. He also had a good number of scars from all the surgeries and tubes. And since he had become mobile and had such poor muscle tone, he was always falling over or bumping into something. No wonder they thought something was up! But I was humiliated, embarrassed, and furious at the very idea they could even think I'd do such a thing. After all we had done to keep him alive?! I gave them all the contact information for his pediatricians and his specialists who could vouch for at least most of his condition. I understood they were just doing their job, but boy was that tough.

Over the course of late spring and through summer, we had at least thirty-seven appointments with doctors, therapists, and clinics of one sort or another. Once summer came, I started babysitting again—this time two of our nieces, Sara and Jessica. And I also started cleaning houses for some extra money as well. That was in addition to trying to garden and keep up with Nathan and all his needs. Life was crazy! We did manage to have a week's vacation with Dave's brother, Rusty, and his family. We went camping at the beach and had a wonderful time!

Nathan really grew up quite a bit over the summer and was maturing in many ways. He was a VERY determined child and was extremely hot tempered! But he was still a beautiful baby. By September Nathan was a little over nineteen pounds. I had begun fooling around with Nathan's diet in an effort to get rid of the tube feedings. It was hard. I had a certain number of calories to get in him in a day and if we were unsuccessful then I had to supplement with tube feedings at night. But after being tube fed all night, Nathan really didn't have much of an appetite during the day. It was a vicious cycle. His creatinine was beginning to creep up mysteriously. The doctors feared his kidneys were beginning to fail. On September 6, Nathan developed another VERY painful hernia and we had to rush him to U.Va. and spent a long evening in the ER. We had outpatient surgery to repair it on October 1. Then on November 4, I was absolutely thrilled to be returning the feeding pump to the hospital! We ended the year the same way we began: lots of appointments with doctors, clinics, therapies, tests, and the like.

Meanwhile, Nathan turned two in December, still small and delayed for his age but an absolute blessing and joy. We were also able to enjoy our usual holiday celebrations with both the Sours and the Coffey families.

Off to School

The New Year brought an exciting development. Nathan began attending the preschool at the Virginia School for the Deaf and Blind for a half day every Friday. He was so small compared to the others, but it was good for his overall development and especially to immerse him in an environment to enhance his sign language skills. Other than preschool, life was relatively calm and "normal" with the usual assortment of medical related appointments.

In April, I had an opportunity to attend a lay renewal weekend at our church, which proved to be a wonderful spiritual growth experience for me and a nice break from my routine.

Nathan began May with a bug of sorts and a very high fever that nothing would bring down. A doctor advised Advil in addition to the Benedryl I was already giving him for his symptoms to help him sleep. I didn't realize that Advil and Benedryl were two big no-no's for renal patients! The medicines in combination almost dried him out to the point of renal failure. We, of course, ended up in the hospital where his creatinine shot up to be only a few tenths of a point away from what was considered renal failure! The nurses had me watching movies and reading material to get me prepared for dialysis. What an intense time!

While we were in the hospital, God gave me a number of scriptures during a very difficult time of uncertainty:

> Isaiah 64:3-4 *³For when you did awesome things that we did not expect, you came down, and the mountains trembled before you. ⁴Since ancient times no one has heard, no ear has perceived, no eye has seen any God besides you, who acts on behalf of those who wait for him.*
>
> 1 Corinthians 2:9 *However, as it is written: "No eye has seen, no ear has heard, no mind has conceived what God*

has prepared for those who love him."

Philippians 4:11-13 *[11] I am not saying this because I am in need, for I have learned to be content whatever the circumstances. [12] I know what it is to be in need, and I know what it is to have plenty. I have learned the secret of being content in any and every situation, whether well fed or hungry, whether living in plenty or in want. [13] I can do everything through him who gives me strength.*

Mark 9:23-24 *[23] "'If you can?'" said Jesus. "Everything is possible for him who believes." [24]Immediately the boy's father exclaimed, "I do believe; help me overcome my unbelief!"*

A friend from church visited and said he felt like he was supposed to give me Psalm 121:

> *[1]I lift up my eyes to the hills—where does my help come from? [2]My help comes from the Lord, the Maker of heaven and earth. [3]He will not let your foot slip— he who watches over you will not slumber; [4]indeed, he who watches over Israel will neither slumber nor sleep. [5]The Lord watches over you—the Lord is your shade at your right hand; [6]the sun will not harm you by day, nor the moon by night. [7]The Lord will keep you from all harm—he will watch over your life; [8]the Lord will watch over your coming and going both now and forevermore.*

Though facing almost certain renal failure, at the last minute Nathan did a turn around and came back to a creatinine of around 2, where he remained stable. What a nightmare! Boy, did I beat myself up over this one! Even though I was simply following instructions, I felt so responsible because I was the one who gave him the meds.

7 Off to School

But God continued to be in control of Nathan's life despite my mistakes and brought him back—again!

In June, we began the process of exploring the preschool options available in our area to address Nathan's educational and especially his developmental needs. We had to explore all our options, even ones that weren't very popular in the opinion of others. Our county public school system offered an Early Childhood Special Education Preschool. Regardless of whether we stayed at VSDB or went with the county preschool, we had to go through an eligibility process that included testing, assessing, and a home interview by a county social worker. Andrea, the preschool teacher, and Joan, the speech therapist, both from Ladd Elementary where Nathan would attend public preschool, came to meet and observe Nathan in his preschool classroom at VSDB. I watched through eyes of scrutiny behind a two-way mirror as they interacted with my little boy in his classroom.

I arranged for Nathan to visit the preschool classroom at Ladd. I was not impressed. There were sixteen preschoolers in the classroom: half of them typically developing and the other half with various handicapping conditions. He was so small compared to the other kids. I was honestly concerned for his safety in the midst of what appeared to me to be total chaos. After our visit, I politely said, "thank you, but no thank you," deciding to keep Nathan at VSDB. Strangely, I never had peace about that decision. My decline actually prompted a phone call from Andrea wanting to talk with me about my decision. I'm not sure exactly what either of us said in the course of that conversation, but afterward, Dave and I decided to give the public preschool a try. We were very nervous, but somehow I had a strange feeling it was the right place for Nathan.

On July 5, my baby girl went to something called "kindergarten in July," an introduction for those starting school in the fall. It was like going to kindergarten but for only a half day for two weeks. What a traumatic experience for me! She did fine for her first day, but as soon as I turned to leave the room, the tears started down my cheeks and then I completely lost it. Over the course of the program, she had several clinging episodes as I dropped her off, but over all she did very well. I just couldn't believe my baby would be starting school that fall!

On July 6, we had an appointment to have another ABR (Audio Brainwave Response) test. After the test was completed, Nathan was waking up from the sedation, sitting on my lap, and looking at a Sesame Street book. We were "reading" the pictures. Nathan was naming the different characters he knew and some of the objects on the pages. He got the attention of the person who had performed the test, who then went and got her supervisor. They both questioned Nathan about his body parts, objects around the room, and the pictures in the book. They were absolutely amazed at his verbal responses. The test they had just performed confirmed the earlier ABR test: severely to profoundly hearing impaired. The results were also in line with the multitude of sound booth tests we had been having routinely performed in order to more accurately identify his exact hearing loss and to identify how well the hearing aids were working and adjusting them accordingly. But they marveled at how a child with such a profound hearing loss could be hearing unaided—yes, I said unaided—and be able to respond to their verbal prompts. They were even more amazed at his ability to verbalize responses to their questions. A deaf child just doesn't do that. Now granted his speech, though intelligible for the most part, was a bit slurred, but that could have easily been because of his poor muscle tone as it was from a hearing loss. They proceeded to conduct another more state-of-the-art test that I fail to remember the name of, and that test was "inconclusive."

We never received an official report from that visit! Our conclusion: God had performed yet another miracle!!! This miracle was confirmed with some of the testing involved in the whole preschool process. According to these tests, Nathan, our severely to profoundly hearing impaired child, was almost on target for his verbal speech and language skills for his age!! God is wonderful! Nathan still had a hearing loss that would need to be aided, especially once he started school during instruction time of any sort. But that was a far cry from hearing nothing when he was a baby and needing sign language as his only mode of communication to being a verbal child both in reception and in communication! I wonder if God in His infinite wisdom knew He needed to intervene and do something about Nathan's hearing when He looked down on that little boy's mother at that silent supper?

On July 8, I was reminded through scripture that sometimes our prayers (such as the prayers for Nathan's hearing) are answered with a "wait":

> John 11:3-6 *³So the sisters sent word to Jesus, "Lord, the one you love is sick." ⁴When he heard this, Jesus said, "This sickness will not end in death. No, it is for God's glory so that God's Son may be glorified through it." ⁵Jesus loved Martha and her sister and Lazarus. ⁶Yet when he heard that Lazarus was sick, he stayed where he was two more days.*

On September 6, both of my children started school—Ashley started kindergarten and Nathan started the ECSE (Early Childhood Special Education) preschool, both at Ladd Elementary. I dropped Nathan off at his classroom first because I figured I'd have a harder time leaving Ashley than him. I was right. I had to leave her crying. I sobbed all the way home as I left both my babies in the hands of people who were practically strangers.

For the next eight weeks—yes, I said eight weeks!—I had to peel my daughter off my leg every morning and leave her crying. At first, I'd cry with her and for her. Then it became tears of frustration. I had several talks with Mrs. Lindsay, her teacher, about Ashley not participating in group activities, like music or games. Mrs. Lindsay even suggested I might want to check out a parenting class about dealing with a strong-willed child! I was certain she hadn't yet met Nathan! I wondered: "If Ashley was truly "strong-willed," then what on earth would that make Nathan?!" We even discussed that maybe she wasn't ready for kindergarten just yet. But in time, she became used to the new routine and slowly began warming up to Mrs. Lindsay, her classmates, and her new environment, and then began to literally thrive!

A little side note on my truly strong-willed child. Practically from birth, Nathan was a very determined little boy. In many respects, it served him well, and I think it was a major part of why he was able to overcome so many obstacles. As a parent trying to discipline him, however, his determination and strong will got the better of me! In addition, Nathan also had a temper. He would get so mad and cry so hard he would get to a point he couldn't catch his breath and would pass out—yes, I said pass out! The first time or two it happened, it scared me to death. Once the shock of it wore off, it became a frustration with me. We eventually learned to blow in his face to help him catch his breath. When that failed and he did pass out, we would sprinkle water on him to wake him up. I truly didn't learn how to parent a medically involved and developmentally delayed child until after he started school. More about that in a bit.

As you remember, it was with major apprehension that we had enrolled Nathan in the public school program, but we agreed to give it a try, somehow feeling it was the "right" thing to do. Well God came through again! What had appeared to be "total" chaos was actually "controlled" chaos and the staff was super! Andrea, "Andy" as the kids called her, was terrific! She was very dedicated to her work and was a Christian. And Diane, the classroom

7 Off to School

aide, was absolutely in love with Nathan! The whole staff (teachers, aides, therapists, and especially the principal, Mr. Chase) thought Nathan was so cute and that he had such a wonderful, engaging personality. You might say Nathan had a knack of somehow wrapping people around his little finger—Mr. Chase being a prime victim to his charm! They all found it quite difficult to discipline him, except for Andy that is. Nathan made lots of progress in all areas, although he still had many motor delays, particularly in walking, sitting, and controlling his upper body. These delays were addressed by Judy, the county's physical therapist. Fine motor skills were also a problem, but we were all working on them and he was making significant progress with the help of his occupational therapist, Martha. The team was rounded out with Joan, the school's speech therapist, to address his ongoing speech and hearing issues. I couldn't have asked for a better group, as professionals or as people, working with my child!

Now back to the issue of Nathan's strong will. On top of everything else that was being addressed at school, Nathan's classroom environment and in particular Andy and the specialists taught me how to parent my strong-willed little boy. The first thing I had to learn was that it was okay to have expectations in spite of the medical conditions and the delays, and it was okay to discipline him. The second thing I had to learn was how to set boundaries and expectations with him that were age and ability appropriate. And the third and perhaps the hardest thing to learn was how to enforce those boundaries and expectations! But in time and with practice, that's just what I did—I became the parent and took charge, while Nathan had to learn to submit to that authority. Not without a good bit of resistance to be sure, but at least we were making progress.

On September 16, Dave and I celebrated our eighth anniversary with a night away. Granddaddy Bill and Grandma Lynn came and stayed with Ashley and Nathan.

It was hard to let go, but we had a wonderful time. Later that month, I went away for a weekend retreat leaving both kids with Dave—another BIG step for me but an absolutely tremendous weekend for me spiritually.

The fall was filled with lots of school related things—field trips, PTA meetings, volunteering in the children's classrooms, and parent conferences. Our medical calendar had even lightened up considerably especially because so many of Nathan's delays, hearing impairment and speech were now being dealt with as part of the preschool program.

Nathan turned three with the usual family celebration. But the real excitement came when he got a power wheels for Christmas. He absolutely loved it! It was a safari jeep that was battery operated. However, we quickly figured out that it was made for sidewalk and pavement driving and not for the terrain of our yard. We returned it for one that had a little more power (typical male!). It was black and yellow and had the name "Big Foot" on the side. I'm going to jump ahead here because I just can't wait until it fits chronologically! Later the following summer, Dave was washing his truck in the yard. Of course, Nathan, three-and-a-half years old at the time, was right along side him washing his own vehicle. Dave's dad, Grandaddy Gordon, came back to the house for a brief chat with Dave and left saying he had to run to Wal-Mart. When Nathan finished washing his vehicle, he hopped in his truck and headed around the side of the house. Dave assumed he was going inside the house. I continued to assume he was with Dave. It seems Nathan had plans of his own. After driving his truck around the house, he then proceeded to head down our 800+/- foot driveway until he got to the main road. Grandma Peggy happened to get a knock on the door from a stranger who was pointing and asking if that was her little boy. Peggy looked and saw Nathan sitting in his Big Foot truck in the middle of the road with traffic stopped both ways. She, of course, flew to Nathan's rescue and personally escorted him back to the house. When asked just what he thought he was doing, Nathan's response was, "Goin' to Wawl-Mawt!" I didn't know whether to laugh or cry! Lord, give me strength!

We had a new addition to the family in December as well. My brother Mike and his wife Audrey had a baby girl. Baby Renea was born with a hernia in her diaphragm and spent the first month of her life in the same NICU that Nathan had. Because of our experience, we were able to relate and answer questions and hopefully offer a little peace of mind. That was something else good that had come out of our circumstances. After surgery and recovery, she was fine and has had no further problems.

Another precious side note, a dear older man in our congregation, Warren Johnson, or "Mr. Jonathan," as Nathan called him, was in the process of getting ready for a liver transplant. His wife Erma shared with me that Warren had told his doctor if he died as a result of his transplant, he wanted Nathan to get his kidney. He loved Nathan that much! Mr. Jonathan did die two weeks or so after his surgery from complications and is sorely missed by many to this day. Unfortunately, Nathan was no where ready for the transplant process, but "Mr. Jonathan's" wishes still touched our hearts.

Nathan Still a Gift of God

Season of Preparation

The New Year started with more frequent doctor appointments for Nathan. I couldn't help but get a little nervous.

In March, we had an Experiencing God weekend at church. I had taken the class the previous summer at church and it was good, but this weekend—Wow! *Experiencing God* is a study by Henry Blackaby and Claude King and is about having a real, personal, intimate relationship with God. Growing up, I had learned a lot of the "stories" of the Bible and to this day love those stories about the different people of the Bible, but I never learned about a personal relationship with God. During one of the testimonies about a "crisis of belief that requires faith and action"[1] (basically, are you going to believe God to the point you act on it), God spoke to me in such a real way—not in an audible voice but in my spirit or in my heart. I felt God say, "I'm not finished with Nathan yet. You've kept me from working through him with YOUR plans, and YOU are assuming I'm finished." I was excited, nervous, and about fifty other emotions all at once! I physically shook and sobbed and then cried again on the way home! Later I was in one of the small group sessions, and the leader turned out to be the same woman that had shared earlier in the day about her crisis of belief. She asked had God spoken to anyone that morning. I didn't speak up—hearing God speak was all so new to me, I wasn't about to share it with a group of people. She asked again and again and each time looked at me! So, I eventually shared. As God would have it, Miss Maggie was also in my small group. She told me later she hadn't really planned on being there but knew she was supposed to be and had actually looked for me. She was pleased to find out we were in the same small group, especially when I shared about God speaking to me. She knew that was why she was supposed to be there. She came back that very night with all sorts of devotional material and tapes saying she felt God wanted me to use them and to also read through the gospels, paying special attention to the healings. Here's an excerpt from Nathan's journal about the weekend:

> God has been speaking and feeding and building my faith and trust by leaps and bounds these last few months!! I'm just so excited about even more yet to come!! I don't know what it means—complete instant healing, gradual healing...I just know something's up even though there's no physical evidence yet. And I also feel God has some work on me yet to accomplish. My prayer life and quiet time and time in God's Word have soared and I just feel so together for the first time in so long!!! After your last hospital stay in May '94 and both of you kids starting school and problems with daddy and me, I suffered a great deal of depression but once again with God's grace I've come through even that! Now I'm just growing in my relationship with God every day and anxiously await what He has in store for me, you, and others around us.

I feel I have to clarify a couple of things from this entry. First, I want to comment on how easy it is to "assume" with God. While I knew God had simply said "He was not finished with Nathan yet" and had not said anything specific about Nathan's healing, I naturally wanted to believe that's what He meant even though that's not what He had said. And in hindsight, I do believe God led Miss Maggie to disciple me in prayer and faith, as well as teach me what the Bible has to say about healing. But as you'll see, I had much to learn about the personal application and processing of it all and even more to learn about the workings of a sovereign God.

Secondly, let me address the statement "problems with daddy and me." Since Ashley had been born, I had been an at-home mom. Dave was the primary provider, although

I did odd jobs to help supplement the family income as I could—babysitting, crafting, and cleaning houses. Dave worked late hours and in the winter would plow snow and do whatever he could to earn some extra money on top of his regular income. Add to the mix a medically involved child and it was almost certain to create stress on our marriage relationship. I was Nathan's primary "nurse," and almost all of the medical care, decisions and responsibilities were left to me. During the early years of his life, Nathan was in and out of the hospital quite a bit. And even when he was home, he had significant medical needs that were often overwhelming. I was tired, lonely, stressed, and too many other things all rolled into one. Dave was stressed with work, tired of having to hold down the fort while I'd be in the hospital, overwhelmed with the financial demands of having a medically involved child, and lonely because even when I was home, I really wasn't home, if you know what I mean.

I can recall on more than one occasion, after I had gotten the kids to bed, sitting in the living room floor in the dark crying and wondering if this would be the night Dave would come home and say he'd had enough, he was done. Both of us were floundering. I thank God He protected us from "others" during this difficult time in our marriage because we both had many voids that were aching to be filled. But in time, especially during Nathan's medical reprieve, we both had a chance to catch our breath and things began to slowly turn around. We both look back on those early days of marriage and shudder to think what we almost lost.

It was at this point that my journaling took a drastic turn. While I still recorded the events of our lives, it became much more about what God was saying to me through His Word. In hindsight, I see much more clearly this was a time of learning, a time of God preparing me for what was yet to come. There were so many scriptures and footnotes from my study Bible that God used to speak to me, too many to include all of them in the body of the story. But my spiritual journey is such an integral part of the story I certainly couldn't leave them out either. So, I am trusting God for guidance in the editing process so that I give a clear account of the journey while not overwhelming the reader with too much detail either.

In the spring of 1995, I had several words from the Lord. Some dealt with healing. In Matthew 9, Jesus asked the blind men who had come to Him for healing, "Do you believe that I am able to do this?"[2] I felt God was asking me if I believed He was able—did I have faith that He could indeed heal Nathan? God also showed me in Acts 3, "It is Jesus' name and the faith that comes through him" that brings complete healing.[3] He also encouraged me through His Word that what we were experiencing would not destroy us[4] but that in fact the Holy Spirit was praying for us.[5] Next came the words that reminded me of the suffering that is inevitable at times for all of us, but with that reminder also came the assurance of His subsequent restoration and healing.[6] Then from a passage in Matthew 14 where Jesus and Peter were walking on water in the midst of a storm, God showed me that we must also go through storms where we will be asked to step out of the boat to test our faith. In the end, even though our own faith (or lack thereof) may cause us to sink, others will still be able to see the hand of God at work in our lives and they will worship Him.[7] Finally by summer, I was encouraged to wait and eventually I would see the Lord's goodness.[8]

Through the story of Jonah making good on his own vow to the Lord, I was reminded of my own promise—a promise I made to God even before Nathan was born—to never turn down an opportunity to share with others what God had done and was doing in our lives.[9] There were also more passages on healing and faith. God showed me that sometimes Jesus was limited in working miracles because of a *lack* of faith on the part of the people.[10] Other stories told of healing coming *because* of a person's faith. The woman's faith was so strong in Matthew 15 that she believed that even the leftovers from Jesus were enough![11] And God again reminded me of the praise that comes from others as they witnessed the healings.[12] But all along, I was still getting messages to "wait" as in the story of Lazarus in John 11.

These messages of healing and faith were mingled with messages of love and hope. A love so great, God gave up His own Son for me.[13] A hope that as God has been there in the past for us, so He would continue to be there in the present and future, always faithful to keep His promises as we persevered through the hard times.[14] God was teaching me that my relationship with Him and my peace in that relationship is based on my faith in His promises. I got a big lesson in faith and holding onto God's promises from the story of Abraham and Sarah in the book of Genesis. God pulled two verses out for me. The first simply said "Abram believed the Lord" and His promise to give him a son which would be the beginning of an entire nation.[15] The second verse recorded the fulfillment of that promise even though it took years to be fulfilled.[16]

The next lesson from the story of Abraham was a little more difficult to hear. As hard as it is to understand sometimes, God tests our faith in order to deepen it and to refine us as persons. In Genesis 22, God asked Abraham to sacrifice the very son they had waited so long for, the son of promise.[17] As hard as I'm sure it was for him, Abraham was willing to be obedient and was at the point of pulling back the knife to follow through with God's command. After seeing Abraham's heart for Him, God Himself provided a ram for the sacrifice. As I endure the testing, I needed to learn to trust in His provision for whatever He calls me to do. God further drove home this point of trusting in Him even when nothing seems to be happening through the story of Rachel, who was married to Abraham's grandson and was also unable to have children. Eventually, "God remembered

Rachel" and opened her womb and she had a son.[18]

Summer ended with more messages on the fact that God's children do have struggles and pain, but those times are also opportunities for growth and developing strong character. In Genesis 35, Jacob wrestled with the angel all night determined not to let go until the angel had blessed him. Talk about a struggle! But Jacob not only got his blessing but his name was changed to Israel. He came away a different person.[19]

Then God took me to the story of Joseph in Genesis chapters 37-50 that tells of Joseph, as a young boy, being sold into slavery. It also tells of how God used Joseph's difficult circumstances to prepare him for a top leadership position in Egypt in order to save God's people from starvation.

Finally, God was teaching me to trust Him in the midst of the trial, even when I could not see an end in sight just as the Israelites had to trust Him even while the "famine was still severe in the land."[20] Or as in the story of the Israelites waiting for God to deliver them from slavery, I, too, had to trust that God would keep His promises to me as well.[21]

On August 28, Ashley started first grade, and Nathan entered his second year in the ECSE preschool at Ladd. Both of them were excelling. Life was somewhat normal for a change at the Sours' household.

With fall, I was also continuing in my own form of school—God's classroom. He wanted me to come to the understanding that the bigger the problem, the bigger was my God who would deliver me with His "outstretched arm and with mighty acts".[22] I was not to let setbacks or delays cause me to doubt God or to turn away from Him. If anything, I needed to draw closer and rely on Him and not myself.[23] I also needed to be determined to follow in obedience, even when He leads in a way that doesn't make sense.[24] And when circumstances seemed to take a turn for the worse, I needed to remember God's faithfulness in the past and have faith and trust in His deliverance knowing just as He delivered the Israelites from Pharoah's army when they were seemingly trapped by the Red Sea, He would also deliver me.[25] In the meantime, I needed to recognize my own helplessness and rely on His comfort in my time of troubles, knowing that one day I would be able to comfort others in their hour of need with what I had received from Him.[26]

In October, we were a bit adventurous as we set out for Savannah, Georgia, to camp for a week, visiting my sister and her husband who were stationed there. We stopped half-way for the night and had a rather uneventful trip. We had a good week actually. We got to see some military things of interest, as well as take a ride on an actual tugboat. The worst thing about the trip was the mosquitoes! Well, that's not quite true. The worst thing about the trip was the ride home — Nathan screamed the entire way, and I do mean the entire nine-ten-hour-drive home, which we made at night "so the kids could sleep!" We wouldn't be making that trip again any time soon!

The year ended with a word that we are being "given over to death" so more of Him may be revealed in our life[27] and an understanding that I was being "refined and tested in the furnace of affliction" for His glory. My suffering was not in vain. It was to grow me more into the image of Christ and to bring Him glory.[28]

Diane, the aide in Nathan's preschool class, was pregnant and needed to go on an earlier maternity leave than expected. Because I was in the classroom volunteering quite a bit and knew the routine, I was asked if I'd like to fill in for her while she was on leave. I agreed and started work on Friday, December 1. It was quite an adjustment being a working mom and another adjustment working in Nathan's classroom. But I truly enjoyed it and found purpose working with all the children, but especially those with special needs or handicapping conditions.

The year ended with the usual holiday activities with

family. Life was full; life was good!

Life's Never Dull

The New Year, 1996, began with a word to the wise to concentrate on the present challenges and responsibilities in order to be prepared for what God has for me in the future. I was also reminded that Jesus prays for my faith to not fail, but when it does, to not give up but turn back to Him.[29]

It was February 12, and I had done a poor job recording the events of our lives. In some respects, we were actually "living" our lives with some sense of relative normalcy for a change. I stopped to make a note regarding Nathan's medical condition. It looked as if we were beginning yet another round of medical involvement. Nathan's kidney function had really decreased in the last year according to his numbers, especially his creatinine level. Through a test, they also discovered he still had some blockage that was causing an unfavorable environment for his kidneys in the present and could cause a problem for a transplant in the future. So they did an outpatient surgery on February 15 to fix that. It was a relatively simple procedure. Dave and I were getting to be ol' pros at this I guess because, once they took Nathan away for surgery, we went and ate lunch while we waited! Everything went fine with the procedure.

God taught me much from the book of Deuteronomy (Yes! The book of Deuteronomy!) through the spring. The book starts out with the startling fact that the Israelites spent forty years on a trip that should have lasted eleven days![30] But God was much more interested in the condition of their hearts than simply bringing them to a new land. They had to be ready to live in that new land. The journey, with its pain and struggle, was the preparation they needed in order to do so. While the Israelites' fear was understandable as they faced the obstacles in the new land, they should not have allowed their fear to control their lives and their choices.[31] They should have moved out in faith trusting God for victory and remembering that sometimes God's workings are a process rather than producing instant results.[32] Deuteronomy 8 revealed that it is the journey that teaches a reliance on God and warns to remember it is God that provides.[33] Chapter 9 warned not to rebel against God's command because of a lack of trust in His provision.[34]

On March 8, Dave and I went on a church sponsored marriage retreat for the weekend. Ashley stayed with Grandaddy Bill and Grandma Lynn while Nathan stayed with Beth and Steve, friends from church. I went with a sinus infection. I was so miserable that Saturday afternoon, during what was to be our free time, Dave took me to see a doctor about getting some medicine. They gave me antibiotics to clear it up, but I had an allergic reaction and by the next morning I was being taken out by stretcher to the local ER. I vaguely remember being put into the ambulance and remember them making a comment about the rash and my breathing. At some point in the ride, they pulled over on the side of the road to start an IV. Dave was following along behind with John and Denise, friends and co-leaders of the retreat. When the ambulance pulled over, they thought something must have happened and Dave even worried that I might have died. I remember waking up in the ER, and my hands and toes were cramping and literally curling. Apparently, they had given me something to counter the reaction. After a few hours, I was released and walked out. We went back and packed up our things and went home. So much for our weekend getaway!

Because we had missed the closing ceremonies of the retreat, everyone from the retreat got together a couple of weeks later so we could have some closure to the weekend. Part of the activities involved an exchanging of "gifts" that somehow symbolized what the weekend had meant to us. I gave Dave an envelope with an old key in it, symbolizing that I learned I needed to be more open and trusting with him and my heart. He, through many tears, gave me an empty envelope, stating that when I was being taken to the hospital and he was fearful I might even die, he realized that his life would be empty without me. Though the marriage retreat itself didn't go exactly as planned, the impact it had on our marriage couldn't have been any better!

April 12, the day we had so hoped to postpone or avoid altogether was here. We went to the transplant clinic. There were lots of tests and so much information to try and process. We also met the transplant doctor who would be performing the surgery. A couple days later, God reminded me that we could be secure in the fact that in the most difficult circumstances, with God, we are able to overcome.[35] God also gave me the assurance that He is with us, even in the fiery furnace.[36]

In May, we had another test to follow up from the surgery in February. They did not get all of the blockage again!!! The doctors would try for a third time, but combine it with the bladder reconstruction surgery. Because of all the damage sustained in utero, Nathan's bladder walls were thickened creating too much pressure for the urinary system, especially the kidneys. With the surgery, they hoped to create a more "friendly" environment for Nathan's future kidney transplant. As part of the procedure, they were going to remove the left kidney and ureter, which was pretty much non-functioning at this point. They would then open up the bladder and, using the tissue from the removed ureter, they would place a "patch" of sorts over the opening in an effort to reduce the pressure inside the bladder. The surgery was scheduled for July 9.

I had an unusually difficult time accepting "here we go again" and went into a really down time mentally, emotionally and spiritually. "WHY?!" I kept tossing that same old question around and around in my mind. I had a real struggle. But with time spent in God's Word and with Him, a series of sermons on faith and a million other little messages from God, I worked through it and accepted once again that Nathan was a "gift from God." I gave him back to God a long time ago to use for His glory, and I have to do it again this time. I finally had peace deep down, although on the outside I was still prone to fall apart. This was confirmed with a passage God gave me on May 23 from Isaiah verses 43:1-3a:

> ¹*But now, this is what the LORD says— he who created you, O Jacob, he who formed you, O Israel: "Fear not, for I have redeemed you; I have summoned you by name; you are mine.* ²*When you pass through the waters, I will be with you; and when you pass through the rivers, they will not sweep over you. When you walk through the fire, you will not be burned; the flames will not set you ablaze.* ³*For I am the LORD, your God, the Holy One of Israel, your Savior.*

On a more positive note, as we were winding down the school year, Nathan had another good year. He had made lots of progress and would return in the fall for one more year in the preschool before moving on to kindergarten. He was cute and knew it! He was a charmer and, at only four years of age, truly knew how to work the system and people to get what he wanted! Everybody loved Nathan! He was such a little pistol! We never knew what he was going to do or say.

Spring brought a family celebration. Dave's brother Mike married Kim on May 18. Nathan was the ring bearer. He was as handsome as could be in his black pants, white shirt and black bow tie! Then spring ended with several words from God. Everything we were going through was all a part of God's plan for us.[37] God knew what the future held as we staked claim to the land He has for us, even the battles that are yet to be fought.[38] I needed to put my faith in God's power, not in the wisdom of man,[39] because God keeps His promises to His children.[40]

With June came swim lessons not only for both kids but for me as well! As a child, I never learned to swim and in fact, had developed quite a fear of water. Because of that, I was determined that my kids would know how to swim. So when I signed them up, I signed myself up as well. Ashley was obviously going to be a natural. She already loved the water and had no fear. Her only problem was that she preferred to swim under the water rather than on top. Nathan was another story. Although he had absolutely no fear of water, he had difficulty floating and controlling his movement in water. His muscle tone was poor and his abdominal cavity had been stretched in utero from the leakage of urine resulting in a rather large "gut." We would tickle or pat his tummy and affectionately refer to him as "buddha belly," to which he grinned and giggled. Anyway, without assistance or "floaties," he sank every time. Amazingly, he didn't seem to mind and would bravely jump in anyway.

I have to take a little detour and share yet another "Nathan story," this one relating to swimming. We had been invited to a pool luncheon with some friends from Ladd. We arrived, and I was busy getting things out of the car and over to the table with strict instructions for the kids to stay away from the pool until they had their floaties on. Seconds, not minutes, SECONDS later, I see Nathan standing on the bottom of the pool just looking up through the water and Andrea reaching in to pull him out. He had used the steps and walked down into the pool and there he stood. Scared me to death! I grabbed him from Andrea and hugged him and cried and squeezed him even tighter!

As for my swim lessons, I managed to complete the two-week beginner's course and earned my certificate by swimming the breaststroke across the deep end of the pool and then the backstroke back across. And that was my last lesson. Though I have been in water since then (usually with a life vest on), I don't know that I could save myself if I had to.

Once we were finished with swim lessons, we took a few days and went camping near Washington, D.C., not only enjoying the activities at the campground but also the zoo, the monuments, and a number of the museums. June ended with two different words from God. First, sometimes God doesn't remove all the difficulties in our lives so that He might develop faith and obedience.[41] In facing those difficulties, God understands our fears, but rather than remove the object of our fear, He often will give us the strength and courage we need to face our fears instead.[42]

Season of Testing

On July 8, 1996, we went through U.Va. admissions in preparation for Nathan's "bladder augmentation," as they were calling it. And with the admission, began another chapter in the continuing saga of Nathan's life. It was nice to see old friends at the hospital, and Nathan of course had fun in "school"—there was a play room and a classroom for children (as their medical conditions allowed) while they were in the hospital to break the monotony of being in a hospital room for hours on end. Nathan had learned to look forward to it after his many stays there. The other thing Nathan had come to love and expect while in the hospital was TV. He loved the Cartoon Network and especially loved to watch Ninja Turtles and Power Rangers—something we didn't get at home. After a rather good time getting settled in, poor Nathan had to end his day with two enemas. Enough said!

The surgery was scheduled for 8 a.m.—we had to be downstairs by 7 a.m. Dave and Pastor Dan met up with Nathan and me just in time to see him go under and be taken back for surgery. I was a bundle of nerves. No matter how hard you try and prepare yourself for these things, it's never easy. I had tried to imagine every possible scenario going into this surgery so I wouldn't be caught off guard. Boy, was I in for the "trip" of a lifetime! (You'll understand my choice of words in a minute.)

Surgery went very well. Even easier than expected. Shorter than expected. No problems or complications. It had been a long day, and we had several visitors, all of whom were amazed and relieved over the events of the day. Dave finally left, tired but happy. I should've known that something was up. Nathan just didn't do things the easy way or without some glitch.

Nathan was groggy but fine considering all that he had been through. Then sometime around midnight, he started itching, and it kept getting worse. They decided it was the drugs he was getting: narcotics through the epidural, opium suppositories, a bladder relaxer, and morphine injections. They gave him some Benedryl for the itching. Then he began to seem uncomfortable with pain, so they gave him some more pain meds. The itching and the squirming turned into startle reflexes. Then the startling turned into jerking motions, especially in his extremities. He then began to have blank stares. Then my baby began having hallucinations of some sort—playing, hitting, and talking to things that weren't there—just generally acting weird. And just when I thought it couldn't get any worse, it did. He began having periods of time where he would have a look of sheer terror on his face. He'd seem to be in a panic and would scream, cry, thrash his body, hold his breath, and then pass out. He did this repeatedly. During this whole fiasco, they played around with his drugs. They stopped the suppositories, and reduced, then finally turned the epidural meds off completely. But they actually increased the morphine, thinking it might relax him. Things only continued to get worse.

 They started a drug called Narcan which counteracts narcotic side effects. It stopped the "fits," but he was still VERY sedated. They stopped the Narcan and the morphine by lunchtime the next day. Then began the most horrible afternoon of my life! The fits returned, only this time they were more like seizures. Through the course of the afternoon, the fits increased in frequency and in intensity. At first, I could handle him and help him through each one. Then it took both myself and my sister to hold him down. (Bec had traveled home just to be with me in the hospital—what a blessing!) Then the mother whose child was in the bed next to Nathan's helped. Everyone was puzzled as to what was happening! The doctors had never seen or heard of anything like this before. They said even children with less renal function than Nathan could handle narcotics, and if there was any trouble, the Narcan fixed it in a couple of hours. The Narcan stopped the fits, but he obviously had a LOT of narcotics stuck in his system. Of course Nathan never did anything according to the books. Sometimes it was almost like he was determined to be different and defy the odds and do things rarely done and seen in the medical world, all to the detriment of his poor mothers sanity!

I was scared. Frantic actually. I sought advice from a friend in the medical field who happened to be there at the time and, on her advice, insisted that Nathan be taken to the PICU where he would receive more specialized attention. The attending resident didn't seem pleased nor did he agree, but I didn't care. Something had to be done for my baby boy! In the PICU, they figured out that as the liver broke down the narcotics and passed them on to the kidney, the kidney was unable to get rid of the byproducts, so they were being reabsorbed into his body. We were caught in a vicious cycle. They decided to use this charcoal-like substance that they use for people who overdose on drugs. It was injected through a tube in his nose into his stomach. It absorbed the narcotics, and then Nathan would either vomit or poop out the charcoal. And boy, what a mess those charcoal treatments were! We had black stuff everywhere! No joke, it took ten or so doses before they thought Nathan was out of the woods! I couldn't believe it! Neither could they.

We were in the PICU from Wednesday until the following Monday when we were finally transferred back to the regular floor. Nathan was finally released on Tuesday. We came home with a supra-pubic tube and urine bag—again! We tried all sorts of bags and ways to accommodate a very mobile child. We even tried a "pee bag" (as we fondly referred to it) that attached to his leg—nothing worked. We finally gave up and simply let Nathan carry the urine bag around with him. Believe it or not, this actually worked very well. He did a pretty good job limiting himself and toting it around with him.

During this time, God had me in the book of 1 Samuel,

reading about another distressed mother—Hannah. Several scriptures spoke to me in the midst of my own very difficult circumstances. The introduction into the book itself stated that "the difficult circumstances in life and the times of waiting often refine, teach, and prepare us for the future responsibilities God has for us"[43]—boy was that ever true! I could see how God had been preparing me for some time for this surgery. Again, God reminded me of His timing and His plan from the story of Hannah who waited "year after year" for a child.[44] Through Hannah's life, He also stressed the importance of prayer in our circumstances and that He has the ultimate control over our lives.[45] And was I ever discovering a truth in the middle of this chaos that "there is no Rock like our God."[46]

God also spoke to me from the life of Samuel. A footnote on Samuel stated that "those whom God finds faithful in small things will be trusted with greater things."[47] Samuel started out helping the priests as a small child and eventually became a prophet of God. God also showed me that all things in life are with purpose—the good, the bad, the small, and the big. He is using them all to lead me to where He wants me to be.[48]

By July 29, Nathan had developed a fever and wasn't feeling well. We took him in and discovered he had a urinary tract infection (UTI) and spent four more days in the hospital for treatment. He finally came home August 1 on an oral antibiotic. The following Friday, we saw Dr. Howards again, and he removed the tube or "tude" as Nathan called it. When Dr. Howards asked Nathan what kind of "tude" it was, Nathan promptly replied "Add-i-toooode!" (Attitude!) We all cracked up! Dr. Howards put him on antibiotics for another five days, because the fever was back. He also said we would need to catheterize Nathan every two to three hours to keep the bladder drained more completely and hopefully prevent infection. What a nightmare that would turn out to be!

10 Season of Testing

Apparently catheterizing Nathan was quite painful, maybe from surgery, maybe because we didn't know what on earth we were doing or maybe both. As we would catheterize him, Nathan screamed; Dave and I cried! It was one of the most horrible things we had had to do to Nathan because of what it was obviously doing to him. The following morning, I arranged with the doctors to get this numbing medication to put on the end of the catheter before we inserted it. I guess it helped, but by then Nathan was already convinced it was going to hurt and was resistant to say the least. And there was this "crook" that we had trouble getting the catheter to thread past, so it seemed to take an eternity to get it in all the way. Once we got it inserted, we would attach a large syringe to the catheter, using it to "suction" out the urine in order to more completely drain the bladder.

Sunday morning was an even bigger disaster with the cathing! Our nerves were raw from the drama of the weekend so far! We were a nervous wreck! Dave and I just lost it! Ashley and Nathan looked at us like we were aliens. Being on auto-pilot, we did what we knew to do on a Sunday morning—we went to church. How we managed that I do not know, but that's what we did. We got to Sunday school and during prayer requests gave a very brief picture of what the events of the last couple days had been like and asked everyone to please pray. Walt Wilson, our church's pastoral counselor, was teaching that day. He later told me the lesson was on something like tithing, and he had no earthly idea how to go from a couple that was obviously on the edge to teaching a lesson on tithing. So he ditched his prepared lesson and turned our lives into a Sunday school lesson on suffering (both from the perspective of those suffering and the perspective of those doing the ministering)! I could've killed him! I felt so selfish that we were the focus of an entire lesson, but others shared later what a blessing it had been. And oh, how the class blessed us! They brought dinners, mowed grass—it was amazing!

The church even arranged for Dave and me to have a night away at a local bed and breakfast the weekend of August 16. It was a lovely B & B! Danny Campbell, our youth pastor, and his wife Elizabeth, who was not only a nurse but a former renal nurse, kept Nathan for us. But we weren't even gone twenty-four hours before we got a call that Nathan had developed a fever. We had to pick him up and take him into the ER, where he got an injection and was then sent home. So much for a break!

We saw Dr. Howards the following Monday, August 19, and he said everything looked fine and we could actually decrease the catheterizing to just at night or as we saw fit. What a responsibility to make that judgment call!

It was interesting how God spoke to me from His Word during this whole catheter fiasco! From 1 Samuel, God showed me it was difficult to trust His timing and difficult to trust Him when the enemy seemed so enormous,[49] but no matter what, God is faithful and trustworthy in any circumstance.[50] And from 1 Peter, I was reassured that my suffering was for a "little while" and my faith was being proved genuine, resulting in praise, glory, and honor as Christ is revealed in my life.[51]

We began getting ready for school, which was to begin Monday, August 26. Nathan was not feeling well. By Friday the 23, we saw a local pediatrician and ended up spending the night in the local hospital with another infection. They sent us home with arrangements for the local home health care nurse to begin injections again. Dr. Castello worked very hard with the pharmacist and the lab to isolate the exact bug and find an antibiotic that would work. They finally determined it was pseudomonas, and there was only one medicine that would fight it. It would require a lot of infusions and a lot of blood work, so they recommended that Nathan get a PIC line, a central line of sorts, that they could access for both giving infusions and for taking blood. The thought was that it would save a lot of sticking and prevent further blowing of Nathan's veins. We were set to get the PIC line on the 27 at U.Va.

Interestingly, the doctor who took care of Nathan in the PICU during his OD episode was the same one who would place the line. Dr. Wilson was such a nice guy! They numbed the site in Nathan's arm where the line was to go in. Dr. Wilson had a tube type instrument about the size of this letter "O," and he was going to insert it into a vein at the bend in Nathan's arm and then thread the line up to his chest area. Well, do I really need to say anymore?! I know I've said it before but this was without a doubt the single most horrible procedure I've been witness to and have participated in! They strapped Nathan down to a bed. Then, I lay across him to help hold his body as still as possible, while they worked on inserting and threading the line. (They would've had a nurse to assist but I knew Nathan would do better if I were there. Plus, I couldn't stand the thought of not being there with him for what I just knew was going to be a difficult procedure.) They worked for over an hour trying to get the line into either arm. The second arm was obviously more painful or maybe less tolerated than the first, even with the numbing medication. The instrument wouldn't thread up the vein in either arm. Nathan screamed and screamed! "No, Mommy! No!" "Please, no Mommy!" "It hurts!" "No, don't Mommy!" Over and over and over. I just kissed his sweet little face and tried to reassure him everything was okay and that it would be over soon and how very sorry I was! Nathan and I were both exhausted and drenched with sweat. At one point, I looked at his sweet yet distressed little face, which was covered with beads of sweat, and in those beads, I saw tiny specs of blood coming out of the pores of his skin. At first, I thought I was seeing things, and quite honestly, it concerned me that something was wrong. But Nathan had screamed so hard and for so long that the little blood vessels in his face had popped. (The medical term for this is "hematidrosis" and yes, it gave a whole new meaning and insight into Jesus' night in the garden![52]) I need not say any more.

They finally gave up. I was whipped physically but even more so emotionally and mentally. To this day, I can still see and hear the whole thing as if it were happening all over again. When they unstrapped Nathan from the table and told him it was all done, he sat up and reached for Dr. Wilson, gave him a big hug, and said, "You're my best buddy!" which brought tears to the doctor's eyes because of all that had just transpired. Because they were unable to insert the PIC line, we ended up doing another plain old IV in his arm. Then, there was discussion of using the same drug we had been using for the past two months! THEN to top it all off, because we were going to use the old drug, we would only have to infuse once every twenty-four hours and only do blood work maybe twice during the whole ten-to-fourteen day treatment! That was the straw that broke the camel's back for me! Boy, was I furious! I had made the decision to put Nathan through that torture for nothing?!!! We were back to old methods being good enough now?!!! I was a wreck to say the least! Here's what I journaled:

> *These past two months have been a living "you-know-what" and now this?! I feel (along with a lot of others) that I'm walking that fine line between sanity and insanity. One more thing and I'll be over the edge. I've felt so distant from God...unable to pray...or very little. I just can't understand "Why?" Such a BIG little word. "Why?" And I still have no answers. I've read "When God Says No" "When Heaven is Silent" and "When God Doesn't Make Sense" searching for comfort and answers. I've come to the conclusion that there are no answers. I simply have to trust God to know what He's doing and have faith He's in control. I have to make the most of what we've got. I had to allow Him to be in control of our lives and all that makes them up. It's what I do with what I have that counts.*

> *I can't waste all my energies on "Why?" and cursing my circumstances. I need to allow God to continue the work He's started. And boy, did it take a long time to get to this point and I still have a long way to go. The story of Job has been a great inspiration to me. A true man of God lost everything...God allowed it. Job never understood but kept faith in God and God restored him. I'm not sure what's around the corner for us or what tomorrow may bring. (Good thing too! I might just run the other way!) But I just have to trust God to know what He's doing.*

During my own "recovery" from the events of the summer, on September 15 God gave me Psalm 30 (Appendix, 1). The words of this Psalm brought me such comfort. I could (and did!) cry out to God, and He would not only hear, but would lift me out of the depths, heal me, turn my wailing into dancing, remove my sackcloth, and clothe me with joy! Wow! God also gave me on the very same day words of conviction regarding my heart, only I didn't understand until a few weeks later the extent of what He was trying to say to me from Ephesians 4:30-32:

> [30] *And do not grieve the Holy Spirit of God, with whom you were sealed for the day of redemption.* [31] *Get rid of all bitterness, rage, and anger, brawling and slander, along with every form of malice.* [32] *Be kind and compassionate to one another, forgiving each other, just as in Christ God forgave you.*

On September 19, God assured me of His concern for me and what we were going through by giving me Psalm 56:8 *Record my lament; list my tears on your scroll—are they not in your record?* God was keeping a record of my tears! And boy, were there a lot of them!

On September 25, I started counseling with Walt, or "Nifty" as he was affectionately known, our pastoral counselor at church. I was not doing well at all. As was typical for me, I had managed to rise to the occasion and do what was needed and demanded of me in the situation but with little regard for myself as a result. I had quite an accumulation of "stuff" that I hadn't really dealt with. Remember that verse from Ephesians 4 about anger and forgiveness? Well, in the course of my working with Nifty, God showed me I was angry. I remember Nifty asking me if I thought I was angry. My response to him was, "No, I don't do anger." He half chuckled and proceeded to give me an "anger" test. Out of a possible twenty-five points, I scored seventeen. I truly thought I had done the test wrong! As we proceeded to talk, Nifty introduced the idea of not only being angry, but my being angry with God. Angry with God?! No way! I grew up believing anger itself was a sin. Even if I were angry, I certainly wouldn't—COULDN'T—be angry with God! But in the course of our working together, I discovered that's exactly what I was—angry with God. Angry for all Nathan and our family had been through, angry for Nathan almost dying over the summer, angry for all the pain I felt God had put us through especially Nathan, angry because we couldn't get a break, but most of all I was angry because it was all out of my control. And you know what? As I began to express and own my anger at God, He didn't strike me dead with a lightning bolt! I discovered my God was big enough to deal with my being angry at Him. Imagine that! Of course, He wasn't going to leave me there, and it was a difficult journey, but how freeing to begin to learn I could be real and honest with God, and He still loved me!

Growing Health Concerns

In our continued effort to have some semblance of normalcy in life, especially for Ashley, we enrolled her in horseback riding lessons. She had more than a passing fancy for horses, and we quickly found out she was a natural in the saddle. Of course, her brother couldn't let his sister get one up on him. So when she would go for lessons he would be allowed to sit in the saddle and be led around on his personal favorite "Batman" with his father or me walking by his side. At one point during the course of Ashley's lessons, Nathan ended up with another infection and had an IV port in his arm for administering antibiotics. Well, Nathan saw no reason why he shouldn't still have his turn on Batman. I was as equally determined that an IV would not prevent him from something he enjoyed. The instructor, on the other hand, did not share our enthusiasm. However, she finally agreed, after we signed a paper saying we accepted full responsibility in the event of a mishap. Yes, we were that determined to have a "normal" life! And Nathan thoroughly enjoyed himself, IV and all!

The fall of '96 also saw the birth of "Nickels for Nathan." Our Ladd family came up with the idea of putting jars in and around school to collect loose change to help with the upcoming costs of transplant. We had insurance, but it would certainly not cover all the expenses, especially the long term care and medications Nathan would need. Plus, who knew how long Dave and I both would be out of work. The students at Ladd were amazing in their sacrificial giving! Some of the kids even gave up snack money or their own allowances for Nathan! The local papers caught wind and began printing articles about Nathan, his miracle birth, and his on-going medical condition. The Ruritans, along with the staff at Ladd Elementary, hosted a spaghetti dinner with a reporter from the local TV station being there. The Nickels for Nathan campaign quickly spread through the community. Individuals, families, churches, businesses, and civic organizations began sending in donations or holding fund raising events and activities of their own with the proceeds going into the Nickels for Nathan Fund. When all was said and done, over $40,000 was raised and placed in a bank account for Nathan's medical expenses! $40,000! That's a lot of nickels! And a lot of reasons for us to be so very grateful to our Ladd family who started it all and to each one who contributed along the way! How truly blessed we were!

Meanwhile, as I continued to read the story of David in the Bible, God had much to say about *His* plans, *His* purposes, and *His* timing versus my own. David had been promised by God he would be king of Israel, but David had to wait for what seemed a long time for that promise to be fulfilled. Plus, in the waiting, David struggled as he faced many trials, but his struggles prepared him for his role as king.

God also spoke to me in my circumstances on October 1 in a profile on Michal, David's wife:

> *We need to see Michal as a person mirroring our own tendencies. How quickly and easily we become bitter with life's unexpected turns. But bitterness only makes a bad situation worse. On the other hand, a willingness to respond to God gives him the opportunity to bring good out of the difficult situations. That willingness has two parts: asking God for his guidance and looking for that guidance in his Word. We are not as responsible for what happens to us as we are for how we respond to our circumstances.*[53]

Also on October 1, I saw that sometimes God says "no" to our plans.[54] I need to trust God for the outcome of the battle.[55] My job is to simply obey.

Then perhaps some of the most sobering words ever jumped up and hit me square in the face from 2 Samuel

12:18:

> *On the seventh day the child died. David's servants were afraid to tell him that the child was dead, for they thought, "While the child was still living, we spoke to David but he would not listen to us. How can we tell him the child is dead? He may do something desperate."*

Children die. In spite of all our prayers and petitions, children die. Again I'm reminded, sometimes God says "no."

October 14, Dave was continuing with the battery of testing as the probable kidney donor for Nathan's transplant. Meanwhile, Nathan was continuing with his own appointments. He started another round of antibiotics, to which he reacted by breaking out in hives, which prompted another visit to the local hospital. And in the midst of it all, I was continuing with my own individual counseling—is there any wonder?!

On November 6, God brought encouragement from Psalm 34:17-19:

> [17]*The righteous cry out, and the Lord hears them; he delivers them from all their troubles.* [18]*The Lord is close to the brokenhearted and saves those who are crushed in spirit.* [19]*A righteous man may have many troubles, but the Lord delivers him from them all.*

Yes, it was reassuring to know God hears, but oh, the knowledge He is close to the brokenhearted and saves those who are crushed in spirit!

By November 11, Nathan was not doing well at all. His creatinine was rising, and I missed a week from work because of his medical situation. By November 21, his creatinine was down somewhat but up again only days later, hitting 4.8, 5.1 then 5.3 by the November 30. The month of December proved to be a wild time with lots of blood work, doctor visits, clinic visits, missed work and school and a variety of medical tests. Somewhere in all the testing, it was discovered that Nathan had contracted CMV (cytomegalovirus), a nasty bug that put a definite halt on moving ahead with a transplant anytime soon, especially because of the anti-rejection medications he would take afterward that would lower his immune system. His creatinine hit 5.8 by December 4, and it looked like we were going to be forced to bite the bullet and go ahead with dialysis—something we were so hoping to avoid. Nathan's health was rather fragile to say the least. With his renal function so poor, we had to be very careful with his diet—try explaining that to a five-year-old! And we had to be especially careful he didn't dehydrate. Not only was his one remaining kidney failing, but Nathan also had trouble concentrating his urine. We walked a tightrope all the time.

With everything going on, I apparently was really searching and needing a "word" from God, because on the 19, I journaled quite a bit from my Bible readings that day. These verses and notes from my study Bible spoke so loudly to me at this time in our lives that I decided to include many of these passages in the body of the story. My hope is that you will see how God was "so there" in the midst of it with us. Very little commentary is needed. The passages speak very clearly for themselves.

First, the profile on Elijah from my study Bible stated that "Elijah witnessed a windstorm, an earthquake and fire. But the Lord was not in any of those powerful things. Instead, God displayed his presence in a gentle whisper." And several random thoughts that struck a chord with me from the same profile. First, "we are never closer to defeat than in our moments of greatest victory." Second, "we are never as alone as we may feel—God is always there." And finally, "God speaks more frequently in persistent whispers than in shouts."[56]

Then, the footnote on 1 Kings 17 and the story of the

11 Growing Health Concerns

widow feeding Elijah in the midst of a famine had this to say:

> *God has help where we least expect it. He provides for us in ways that go beyond our narrow definitions or expectations. No matter how bitter our trials or how seemingly hopeless our situation, we should look for God's caring touch. We may find his providence in some strange places! The widow thought she was preparing her last meal. But a simple act of faith produced a miracle. She trusted Elijah and gave all she had to eat to him. Faith is the step between promise and assurance. Miracles seem so out of reach for our feeble faith. But every miracle, large or small, begins with an act of obedience. We may not see the solution until we take the first step of faith. Even when God has done a miracle in our lives, our troubles may not be over. The famine was a terrible experience but the worst was yet to come. God's provision is never given in order to let us rest upon it. We need to depend on him as each new trial faces us.*[57]

Next was the prayer of Elijah found in 1 Kings 18:36-38:

> [36]*At the time of sacrifice, the prophet Elijah stepped forward and prayed: "O Lord, God of Abraham, Isaac and Israel, let it be known today that you are God in Israel and that I am your servant and have done all these things at your command.* [37]*Answer me, O Lord, answer me, so these people will know that you, O Lord, are God, and that you are turning their hearts back again."* [38]*Then the fire of the Lord fell and burned up the sacrifice, the wood, the stones and the soil, and also licked up the water in the trench.*

The footnote added *Like Elijah, we can have faith that whatever God commands us to do, he will provide what we need to carry it through.*[58]

And finally God spoke to me through, 1 Kings 19:3:

Elijah was afraid and ran for his life. When he came to Beersheba in Judah, he left his servant there with the footnote adding:

> *Elijah experienced the depths of fatigue and discouragement just after his two great spiritual victories: the defeat of the prophets of Baal and the answered prayer for rain. Often discouragement sets in after great spiritual experiences, especially those requiring physical effort or involving great emotion. To lead him out of depression God first let Elijah rest and eat. Then God confronted him with the need to return to his mission—to speak God's words in Israel. Elijah's battles were not over; there was still work for him to do. When you feel let down after a great spiritual experience, remember that God's purpose for your life is not yet over.*[59]

On November 27, I was reading the story of the servant girl who informed her master Naaman that Elisha the prophet could heal his leprosy.[60] Like the servant girl, I needed to be obedient where God has placed me. I also needed to learn a lesson from Naaman and be obedient to whatever God asks of me, no matter how ridiculous it may seem.

Nathan ended up spending the night in the hospital on November 30 and started another antibiotic for a UTI. His creatinine continued to be all over the place. On December 2—Nathan's fifth birthday—God encouraged me with a much needed word from 2 Kings 6:16-17:

> [16]*"Don't be afraid," the prophet answered. "Those who are with us are more than those who are with them."* [17]*And Elisha prayed, "O Lord, open his eyes so he may see." Then the Lord opened the servant's eyes, and he looked and saw the hills full of horses and chariots of fire all around Elisha.*

The footnote added:

> *Elisha's servant was no longer afraid when he saw God's mighty heavenly army. Faith reveals that God is doing more for his people than we can ever realize through sight alone. When you face difficulties that seem insurmountable, remember that spiritual resources are there even if you can't see them. Look through the eyes of faith and let God show you his resources. If you don't see God working in your life, the problem may be your spiritual eyesight, not God's power.[61]*

Also on the same day, God encouraged me through the story of a severe famine to have faith and to trust Him even when in the middle of seemingly impossible circumstances.[62]

And somehow even in the midst of all the medical chaos and stress, we managed to enjoy the holidays as much as we possibly could with such a sick little boy. We continued to be determined to make the most of any given situation squeezing every bit of life and joy out of every moment that we possibly could. Though, admittedly it was getting harder and harder given the uncertain circumstances we faced on a daily basis.

Nathan Still a Gift of God

No Other Option

My journaling dropped off significantly during the first five or so months of 1997. I was too busy trying to stay one step ahead of Nathan! The New Year began much as the old one ended: lots of blood work, doctor visits, tests and missing school, and missing work.

It wasn't until June 18 that I made an entry—a very interesting entry given what we were facing. I was in 2 Chronicles 7 where Solomon was dedicating the temple.[63] I sensed God was asking me to dedicate my "temple" or my life as set apart for His purposes. I also felt He was asking me to do the same with Nathan as well. I did it, but I can't say it was without fear and trembling. A later passage in chapter 9 tells the story of the Queen of Sheba coming to visit King Solomon because of all she had heard of him. It reminded me that our lives are a witness before others.[64]

The next day I didn't have too much trouble swallowing the truth I found in my reading, I was already living it! The reality that when times are tough, I draw closer to God, and when things are going well, I tend to become complacent in my relationship with Him.[65] Sad but true, and at this point, I felt like I was holding on for dear life!

But on June 21, my readings were a little harder to receive. Our obedience and faithfulness are rewarded though sometimes not here on earth but in Heaven.[66] I also received a warning that once I've sought God on something, I then needed to follow His instruction once I received it.[67] And I finally was reminded of God's sovereignty over all situations including what was going on with Nathan.[68]

June 30 brought the insight that in order for my strengths and abilities to be of the greatest use, they needed to be under God's control and influence. God also gave me a word to the wise on July 2 that difficult times can either destroy a person or grow a person.[69] The very next day God showed me through reading about Hezekiah as he was facing an invasion by his enemy that whatever I face, I need to do what I can do and trust God for the rest and for the outcome.[70] There was also the reminder that God is on my side.[71]

On July 4, Independence Day interestingly enough, God reminded me that the key to freedom in any situation is not just hearing His Word, but obeying what it says.

On July 9, Dave and I took Nathan to Duke University for a second opinion. Nathan's creatinine was soaring, his health deteriorating, and we could no longer prolong a decision about dialysis. We (especially I) just had to be sure we were doing the right thing, that we weren't missing something. Once we went on dialysis, there was no turning back. Duke only confirmed the path we were on with U.Va. The trip for a second opinion was unnecessary maybe, but the confirmation gave me what I needed—the peace and assurance that we had no other option but to start dialysis. Surgery to prepare Nathan for dialysis was scheduled for August 19.

On July 15, I realized anew my hunger and need for God's Word in my life, especially in the midst of our circumstances. Then on July 16, God spoke a very profound word to me regarding my fears about moving forward with dialysis. I needed to pray telling God how I was feeling and then take the necessary action trusting He would do His part in the process.[72]

The month of July continued with instruction from God's Word. As I continued my reading in the book of Nehemiah, I was encouraged to pray and reminded that I needed to continue to ask God for help being ready to act as He directs. I had to guard my weaknesses. And as I began reading the book of Esther I saw that even as I questioned the circumstances, I still had to trust that God is in control.

On July 23, Nathan had several appointments in preparation for surgery. His creatinine was now 7.3. A couple days later on July 25, from the life of King Xerxes in the book of Esther, God showed me that I needed to base my decisions on careful thinking rather than on the emotion of the moment.[73]

God ended the month of July with another word from the book of Esther. Basically, God can be trusted as He works in the circumstances in our lives no matter what they may seem from our view point. On the same day, I was also shown that there are no "coincidences" with God. He was carefully working together all the details of our lives for good just as He did in the life of Esther.[74]

Call us insane, but July 28 we packed up the camper and headed to Williamsburg for a long weekend—one last hoorah before surgery and life drastically changed forever. We ended up in the ER of the town on the 30th—of course! Thankfully, we were used to this by now, and we had scouted out the location of the local hospital upon pulling into town "just in case." Nathan spiked a fever in the middle of the night, and we packed everyone up—scooping Ashley out of bed with her blanket and pillow. Believe it or not, we managed to cart her to the hospital, get her onto a couch in the ER waiting room, back into the vehicle, back to the campground, into the camper, and she never knew a thing! AMAZING! It took much longer being in a facility where the staff didn't know Nathan and so of course they wouldn't take my word as to what needed to be done. It took a bit for them to confirm with U.Va., but eventually they did and we were on our way. Despite the "unexpected" tour of the local hospital, we really did have a wonderful weekend. As we were leaving, I was reminded AGAIN from the book of Esther that God is in control. With that, it was time to get back to reality.

On August 6 as we were facing dialysis surgery, God took me to the book of Job of all places! Given the gravity of what we were facing, God's timing was perfect with the messages He brought through the story of Job. He also spoke to me from the profile on the book of Job from my study Bible:

> *His (God's) will is perfect, yet he doesn't always act in ways that we understand. We should serve God for who he is, not what we feel. We must be careful not to judge others who are suffering. We may be demonstrating the sin of pride. We must be cautious in maintaining the certainty of our own conclusions about how God treats us. He (Job) never placed his hope in his experience, his wisdom, his friends, or his wealth. Job focused on God. When everything is stripped away, we are to recognize that God is all we ever really had. We must remember that this life, with all its pain is not our final destiny.*[75]

Then Job 1:1: *In the land of Uz there lived a man whose name was Job. This man was blameless and upright; he feared God and shunned evil.* From the beginning of the book of Job to its end, Job is left with never understanding why he lost everything. He doesn't even have the privilege we do of knowing the conversation between God and Satan. Like Job, we often find ourselves in the middle of difficult circumstances asking, "Why?" Will I then be like Job and allow the circumstances to grow my faith as I trust God through them?

Also on August 6, Job 1:8, 12:

> [8]*Then the Lord said to Satan, "Have you considered my servant Job? There is no one on earth like him; he is blameless and upright, a man who fears God and shuns evil."* [12]*The Lord said to Satan, "Very well, then, everything he has is in your hands, but on the man himself do not lay a finger." Then Satan went out from the presence of the Lord.*

It's hard to think God would dangle "His servant" in front of Satan that way but He did. God knew Job and knew what he could handle. God also knows us and allows things in our lives to grow us and come to a place like Job eventually does where we know God in a more intimate way.

12 No Other Option

On August 7, I read the Bible's written record of Job's response to his disaster in Job 3. Job basically cursed the day he was born given his present set of circumstances where he had lost everything. To me, it was freeing in that it gave me permission to cry out to God and tell Him exactly how I was feeling in my own set of circumstances.

On August 11, as we were doing final testing and had numerous doctor appointments in preparation for surgery, I continued reading of Job's agony in Job 6:1-4:

> *¹Then Job replied: ²"If only my anguish could be weighed and all my misery be placed on the scales! ³It would surely outweigh the sand of the seas—no wonder my words have been impetuous. ⁴The arrows of the Almighty are in me, my spirit drinks in their poison; God's terrors are marshaled against me.*

Boy, did that ever describe how I was feeling!

On August 12, we did it again! We gave into insanity and packed the camper up and headed over to a local campground only minutes from the house for the weekend. Nuts? Maybe. Regrets? None!

On August 13, God spoke to me through Job 12:24-25: *He deprives the leaders of the earth of their reason; he sends them wandering through a trackless waste. They grope in darkness with no light; he makes them stagger like drunkards.* Sometimes God's ways are so contrary to the logic of man!

August 19, the dreaded day, had arrived. Surgery was scheduled for 8 a.m. Surgery went well. We had decided to go with peritoneal dialysis. Nathan would have a tube that tunneled under the skin on his tummy and then into the abdominal cavity. We would hook him up to a machine at bedtime that would pump fluid into his abdomen. The fluid would pull toxins off his organs and then the machine would "suck" out the bad fluid and pump more clean fluid back in. This would cycle multiple times in the course of the night, and then we would unhook him from the machine in the morning. One of the biggest benefits was that it can be done at home while Nathan slept. I couldn't imagine trying to do hemodialysis with him! Sitting for hours three to four times per week to a machine that filters the blood?! But the one downside with peritoneal was the risk of infection, particularly a tunnel infection (the sight where the tube entered his tummy), so learning the proper technique to prevent infection was critical.

It took awhile for them to get the amount of fluid and timings of the cycle and the machine regulated to fit Nathan. But believe it or not, we were home by the August 26. But it was short lived. We went back in on August 27 with complications with the machine and were in the hospital for two more nights. But Nathan actually was able to start school on September 4. I took a little time for myself and didn't go back until Monday the 8th. It was on that day that I found Job 21:22: *Can anyone teach knowledge to God, since he judges even the highest?*

Mrs. Elliott, Nathan's kindergarten teacher, was more than a little nervous about having a very active, albeit clumsy, little boy with a tube coming out of his tummy that needed to be protected at all times from moisture and most of all from getting hit or banged with any force. It took a team of innovative people to come up with a "belt" to protect his tube site. It was made of lightweight molded plastic and it fit over the tube site to protect it from harm. It was much like the turtle shells the Teenage Mutant Ninja Turtles wore only Nathan wore this on his tummy instead of his back! It wasn't the most attractive, but it served the purpose. Rather than be embarrassed or feel awkward about his contraption, Nathan was quite proud. The only thing that bothered him was that it slowed him down getting to the playground because of the time it took to harness him up in it! All in all, we adjusted rather well to life with dialysis. But it sure was a lot of work and even more responsibility.

12 No Other Option

Our smooth sailing didn't last long. By September 15, he had another UTI and started antibiotics for ten days. Nathan's favorite renal nurse, "Nuhrse Fuhrn" (Nurse Fern) came for a visit at school to discuss Nathan's health care plan and then a home visit to see how we were handling the dialysis at home. God bless people like Nurse Fern! She had been making our situation bearable since Nathan's birth. She patiently answered questions, calmed a mother's nerves more than once and always smiled as she dealt with a very active little boy!

God's word to me on October 3 stung. 1 Timothy 6:6 *But godliness with contentment is great gain.* Contentment? In the middle of this? God would have to take care of this one—it was all I could do to survive. On October 4, I was reminded of God's trustworthiness.[76]

As I continued reading in the book of Job, I was still very much identifying with the struggle to know why God allows things into our lives. On October 19, God spoke to me from Job 38:1: *The Lord answered Job out of the storm* with the footnote adding: *Our only option is to submit to his authority and rest in his care. During difficult times, we too must humbly remember our position before the eternal holy incomprehensible God.*[77]

On October 24, some very familiar verses in Lamentations reminded me that though God "brings grief," I am not consumed because His "compassions never fail." Great is His faithfulness as I wait and hope in Him.[78]

On October 26, Job 42:1-6 spoke to me:

> *¹Then Job replied to the Lord: ²"I know that you can do all things; no plan of yours can be thwarted. ³You asked, 'Who is this that obscures my counsel without knowledge?' Surely I spoke of things I did not understand, things too wonderful for me to know. ⁴"You said, 'Listen now, and I will speak; I will question you, and you shall answer me.' ⁵My ears had heard of you but now my eyes have seen you.*

> *⁶Therefore I despise myself and repent in dust and ashes."*

The footnote on the passage added:

> *He did not ask for forgiveness for committing secret sins, but for questioning God's sovereignty and justice. Job repented of his attitude and acknowledged God's great power and perfect justice. We sin when we angrily ask "If God is in control how could he let this happen?" Are you using what you can't understand as an excuse for your lack of trust? Admit to God that you don't even have enough faith to trust him. True faith begins in such humility.*[79]

Also on the 26, I read Job 42:17: *And so he died, old and full of years.* Job died never knowing why God had allowed the incredible loss in his life but he died trusting God with those unanswered questions and died having lived a full life.

On November 7, Psalm 13:1 was like reading my own words: *How long, O Lord? Will you forget me forever? How long will you hide your face from me?*

On November 10, I saw I could still have joy in the midst of my circumstances from Psalm 16:9: *Therefore my heart is glad and my tongue rejoices; my body also will rest secure.*

On Saturday, November 22, I had hired a babysitter for the day so I could go shopping with the girls in my family at Potomac Mills. While I was there, "something" said I needed to call home. When I did, I discovered Nathan had spiked a fever. I spoke with Dave, who agreed to take him to the ER at U.Va., and I would meet him there. We won't talk about how fast I made the trip from northern Virginia to Charlottesville! It seems Nathan had come down with strep and another UTI (or perhaps still the same one), and we ended up being admitted and stayed for a couple days until they could get both under control.

We still managed to enjoy the holidays. For his birthday and Christmas, Nathan got a bunch of boy toys—super

12 No Other Option

heroes and action figures. He was obviously growing up because the pieces had significantly decreased in size but increased in number.

Preparing for Transplant

Well, it happened. The thing we tried our best to avoid because of all the horror stories we had heard about them—Nathan got a tunnel infection which meant the site where the dialysis tube "tunneled" under the skin and into Nathan's abdominal cavity had gotten infected. We went in the hospital on January 3, 1998, for a couple of nights. We came home on two potent antibiotics that we were to run through the end of the month.

As I felt like I was drowning in it all, God gave me a passage in Psalm 18:16: *He reached down from on high and took hold of me; he drew me out of deep waters.* Did I ever need Him to pull me out as I felt like I was drowning much of the time! In addition, He reminded me that He is my strength and would enable me to stand and do battle.[80] I needed to keep my trust in Him and Him alone.[81]

Then on January 12, the idea of "death" was again in my face with the well known passage from Psalm 23:4: *Even though I walk through the valley of the shadow of death, I will fear no evil, for you are with me; your rod and your staff, they comfort me.* I was reassured that even then, He is with me.

On January 18, a number of passages spoke to me from the Psalms. I was assured God is my refuge and hope when I am feeling "lonely and afflicted."[82] I could also be confident the Lord would be my "light and salvation" when I was afraid [83] and I could be "strong and take heart" as I waited for Him. [84]

On January 23, the Psalms seemed to speak a great deal, especially Psalm 30, which had spoken vividly to me before (Appendix, 1) and Psalm 31 (Appendix, 2). Both Psalms speak of times of great struggle: a time of "going down into the pit," of an "anguish of my soul," of being "consumed by anguish" and of "strength failing because of my affliction and bones growing weak." But both Psalms also offer hope that God will "turn my wailing into dancing and remove my sackcloth and clothe me with joy" and He will "show His wonderful love to me in a besieged city." God does not always deliver FROM a trial or a circumstance, but He will ALWAYS be there in it with me and see me through it.

February 5 brought news of another UTI and more antibiotics, and on February 12, God spoke specifically to me from His word regarding our circumstances. First Psalm 35:13: *Yet when they were ill, I put on sackcloth and humbled myself with fasting. When my prayers returned to me unanswered.* And then Psalm 37:4-5: *Delight yourself in the Lord and he will give you the desires of your heart. Commit your way to the Lord; trust in him and he will do this.* We had been battling illness in one fashion or another with Nathan for years and it certainly was the desire of my (our) heart for him to be healed. It was frustrating at times because it appeared our prayers were unanswered—we were not being given the desires of our heart. Why wasn't he healed? How could God not answer the prayer of a little boy who at bedtime would ask in his childlike way, *"Dear 'Geez-shush' please make my 'kit-a-knees' better so we don't have to do 'chans-plant'"* (Translated: Dear Jesus, Please make my kidneys better so we don't have to do transplant.) And "Geez-shush" said, "No." Of course, it causes you at times to doubt your own faith—maybe I don't have faith enough to move this mountain or maybe I'm not praying right, maybe I have unconfessed sin in my life. We make seemingly "unanswered" prayers about us. Sometimes it's not about us at all but has everything to do with God and His will and His timing. In those times, I keep praying and asking for healing, but I have to eventually trust God and know that His ways are not my ways. I needed to wait and trust God to hear my cry and lift me out of the slimy pit and set my feet on a rock, and as a result, many will see and put their trust in the Lord as well.[85]

On February 27, my focus was shifted off myself and toward God as I continued reading in the Psalms. I saw Him as my "refuge and strength, an ever-present help in

13 Preparing for Transplant

trouble,"[86] as "awesome, Lord Most High and the great King over all the earth,"[87] and as being eternal and my "guide to the end."[88]

On March 12, I went to dinner and coffee with my sister-in-law Tammy. She and I had gotten to be rather close over the years, close enough to have a very difficult and odd conversation, even for us. It took a bit to get up the courage to broach the subject, but I finally was able to voice my concerns that I felt like God was preparing me for Nathan to die. This was the first time I had verbalized what I had been sensing and wrestling with for some time. Quite honestly I expected, and even hoped, she would respond with a strong rebuttal. She didn't. In fact, she shared she had been having the same thoughts. It was good to finally speak my thoughts, but at the same time, it seemed our conversation made it all too real.

Just a few days later on March 19, I was back to the idea of "death" and the sense of it looming on the horizon. It wasn't your typical pessimism because of our circumstances but a real sense of it being impending. And it wasn't that I happened to be in a passage about death and then jumped to the conclusion it must be a "sign." To be quite frank, I felt God had been speaking to me of what was to come and He was only confirming it through His Word. But it was so much more than gaining a sense of "knowing." That wasn't the point. More and more I saw God preparing me in advance for what was coming so I'd be ready for the battle as in Psalm 55:4-8, 16-19, 22:

> [4]*My heart is in anguish within me; the terrors of death assail me.* [5]*Fear and trembling have beset me; horror has overwhelmed me.* [6]*I said, "Oh, that I had the wings of a dove! I would fly away and be at rest—*[7]*I would flee far away and stay in the desert; "Selah"* [8]*I would hurry to my place of shelter, far from the tempest and storm."* [16]*But I call to God, and the Lord saves me.* [17]*Evening, morning*

> *and noon I cry out in distress, and he hears my voice. ¹⁸He ransoms me unharmed from the battle waged against me, even though many oppose me. ¹⁹God, who is enthroned forever, will hear them and afflict them—"Selah" men who never change their ways and have no fear of God. ²²Cast your cares on the Lord and he will sustain you; he will never let the righteous fall.*

In all my fears, I was to trust Him, trust Him and not be afraid.⁸⁹ Some things just had to be drilled into me!

On March 20, we had a visit to the transplant clinic. On March 25, Nathan had yet another UTI and was prescribed more antibiotics.

On March 31, in a few short verses from Psalm 62 I learned of God as my rest, my salvation, my rock, my fortress, my hope and my refuge.⁹⁰

On April 5, I took Nathan to the ER and started ANOTHER round of antibiotics for infection.

In mid-April, we went to Kings Dominion. The kids had a ball, especially Nathan. However, he was more than a little upset and didn't understand why his sister got to ride the "big" rides and he didn't. Even though at heart Nathan was more than adventurous and truly knew no fear, he was too short for many of the rides. We did manage to get him on a roller coaster that had enough twists and turns to at least quiet the protests. We also took him on the flume ride, which seemed a little more exciting than some of the "kiddie" rides to Nathan. It probably was not the wisest thing for someone with a dialysis tube in their tummy and certainly not something we would advise but that's the way of the Sours! We padded the tube site with a towel and taped several layers of plastic garbage bags around his tummy in order to keep the site from getting bumped and to keep it dry. Quite a bit of effort to have some fun but worth every bit of it!

On April 29, I again saw how God tests and refines us

13 Preparing for Transplant

but eventually brings us out.[91]

Sadly, Dave's Grandma, fondly known as "Grandma Pickie", died and was buried on May 2. How she loved Nathan! She and her home-cooked meals are missed to this day!

On May 8, Dave had his arteriogram in preparation for transplant. This test provides a look at the blood flow into Dave's kidney that will become Nathan's, making sure there are no potential problems. It required Dave to have a large tube inserted in the artery in his groin and threaded up to the kidney. Then they injected dye so they could follow the blood flow. The hardest part of the whole procedure was lying completely flat on his back for the several hours afterward. Not a pleasant experience to be sure for either one of us! But a proud moment as I was witness to the sacrifice my husband was gladly making for his son! Everything checked out okay, and one more hurdle was out of the way for doing a transplant.

That same day God reminded me again to remember His faithfulness in the past in order to trust Him in the present. It may mean a trip through the Valley of Baca (or valley of weeping), but the journey will provide two things. One, the journey leads you to a deeper relationship with God, and secondly, the journey will provide springs of refreshing for those traveling after you.[92]

The Psalms continued to bring encouragement in mid-May but also brought some sobering words about the need to be encouraged in very difficult circumstances. I was encouraged that God's faithful love would be with me, and through Him I would do what He called me to.[93] Without His help, death would silence me. His love will support me, and He will bring me joy in the midst of my anxiety.[94] I needed to be on guard against my heart becoming hard in the desert.[95]

Because of all of the problems with infections, we started an antiseptic bladder flushing on May 21 as a safeguard in preparation for transplant. God brought me a word to the wise to not be a lone ranger as we go through this but to reach out and accept the help and support of family and friends.[96] On May 22, Dave gave blood in case he might need it during surgery.

On May 31, I felt God was saying the surgery may be part of something He is using to prepare me for the future somehow.[97]

On June 1, I'm again reminded of the Lord's "mighty acts" not just Biblically but in my own life.[98] In spite of God's preparation for what's to come, I'm still praying for yet another mighty act for Nathan. However, I'm to pray God's will be done, trusting He knows best even when it means He allows trouble in our lives. My time with God ended that day with a verse about praising God from Psalm 107[99] and a sobering footnote:

> *Those who have never truly suffered may not appreciate God as much as those who have matured under hardship. Those who have seen God work in times of distress have a deeper insight into his loving-kindness. If you have experienced great trials, you have the potential for great praise*[100]

Also on June 1, Nathan had an EKG, an x-ray, started antibiotics, and had a final visit to the renal clinic. We then had a final verification on the cross match for Dave as Nathan's donor. Could we possibly be down to the wire like this?

As a last family hoorah (you know us and our last hoorahs!) on June 2, we kept Ashley out of school, and we went to the park and let the kids play on the equipment and feed the ducks. We let Nathan choose where we had lunch. He chose a local drive-in restaurant that served the kids meal in a box shaped like a car—no surprise! We had a good time but oh, the cloud that hung over us that day—in particular,

13 Preparing for Transplant

the one over my heart. Everyone knew of the "elephant" in the room but tried so hard to pretend it wasn't there or at least that it wasn't such a big deal.

On Wednesday, June 3, Nathan was to be admitted a day before the transplant surgery. I was busy getting all the last minute details taken care of at home. We were anticipating a lengthy stay for Nathan. I had no idea when I'd be back home. As I made Nathan's bed, a strange feeling came over me and in the same instance I "knew" this would be the last time I would ever make his bed. I quickly shook that feeling off and out! What a terrible thing to be thinking!

Nathan was actually looking forward to his trip to the hospital. He knew it meant "going to school," playing in the playroom and watching Power Rangers on TV. He showed no concern for what lay ahead. Thank God for small favors! I'm not sure what I would have done if I had to do battle to get him there. Once there, we had all the prep for surgery we could stand. That evening Dave came over with Ashley, and we all enjoyed pizza, per Nathan's request of course. Again, it was a good time together, but that cloud just wouldn't lift. Dave and Ashley finally went home—Dave was looking at an early trip over in the morning with his parents, and Nathan needed to go down for the night as well.

I was left up alone. Unable to sleep. Restless. I read my Bible a lot, continuing in the Psalms. They continued to speak to me about God and who He is. Just being in His presence causes us to tremble.[101] Another verse reminded me God remembers us even though we may feel alone or abandoned by Him.[102] They also continued to speak to me about the "cords of death" and being "overcome by trouble and sorrow."[103] As if that wasn't enough, I was blown away by Psalm 116:15: *Precious in the sight of the Lord is the death of his saints.* The related footnote was also a kicker:

> God stays close to us even in death. When someone we love is nearing death, we may become angry and feel abandoned.

> *But believers are precious to God, and he carefully chooses the time when they will be called into his presence. Let this truth provide comfort when you've lost a loved one. God sees and each life is valuable to him.*[104]

That was followed by the instruction to "take refuge in the Lord"[105] with a footnote that asked if I was *"willing to trust God to guide you here on earth and to your eternal destination? Do you trust him more than any human being? How futile it is to trust anything or anyone more than God.*[106] Psalm 118:24 says, *This is the day the Lord has made; let us rejoice and be glad in it.* The footnote on that verse spoke to me as well, stating:

> *There are days when the last thing we want to do is rejoice. Our mood is down, our situation is out of hand, and our sorrow or guilt is overwhelming. We can relate to the writers of the Psalms who often felt this way. But no matter how low the psalmists felt, they were always honest with God. And as they talked to God their prayers ended in praise. When you don't feel like rejoicing, tell God how you truly feel. You will find that God will give you a reason to rejoice. God has given you this day to live and to serve him—be glad.*[107]

My last journal entry on June 3 before attempting to sleep was Psalm 112:4, 7-9:

> *Even in darkness light dawns for the upright, for the gracious and compassionate and righteous man. He will have no fear of bad news; his heart is steadfast, trusting in the Lord. His heart is secure, he will have no fear; in the end he will look in triumph on his foes. He has scattered abroad his gifts to the poor, his righteousness endures forever; his horn will be lifted high in honor.*

13 Preparing for Transplant

The footnote added:

> *To fear God means to respect and revere him as the almighty Lord. When we trust God completely to take care of us, we will find that our other fears—even of death itself—will subside.*[108]

And then sometime after midnight I simply wrote in my journal:

June 4: Dave comes in the morning.

Nathan Still a Gift of God

Our Worst Nightmare

And Dave did indeed come in the morning along with his parents. Nathan and I met them downstairs in the surgical unit. I was a mess internally but kept the face on for everyone else's sake. I just couldn't shake this "feeling." Pastor Dan was there with us, of course. I held Nathan. We made light talk—strange how you feel a need to do that when everyone in the room has only one thing on their minds. They finally came to put Nathan under in typical fashion—with the "mask." Nathan was an ol' pro and of course knew what was up at this point and began to protest, "No, not the mask! Not the mask!" I held him even tighter and tried to reassure him. They managed to get it close enough to his face that it began to take effect, and he eventually went limp in my arms which only heightened the "feeling" I was having. Once he was completely out, we kissed on him and loved on him, and the nurses took him from me to get him prepped for surgery. We were all shooed out of the room. I was the last one to leave. I turned and looked back as I walked through the door. I saw the nurse with Nathan in her arms quickly whisking him away. Every ounce of my being wanted to run back in and take him from her and just forget this whole thing! But that was absurd! We knew this was the right thing to do. Transplant was what would give Nathan a shot at a "normal" life, right? We had even confirmed it with another hospital. Even "knowing" it was the "right" thing, I somehow dreaded what was just set into motion. There was no turning back now. I turned, and the door closed behind me. Oh, what a sick feeling! One that could not be shaken.

The surgery was hours long. Throughout the course of the day, so many different people showed up to wish us well and encourage us, to let us know they were there and praying for us. I found out some were even fasting for us. Dave's dad couldn't stand the stress and gave up his recent decision to stop smoking. It just wasn't the day for that kind of will power! We finally got word that the surgery was over. Everything had gone well and both were doing fine. They said as soon as they hooked up Nathan's new kidney, it started producing urine—a very good sign indeed! Maybe I was worried for nothing.

After the surgery was over, we couldn't figure out where they had taken Nathan, so Peggy and Mary Jane set out on a scouting expedition. No doubt they would not return until they had some answers! They did indeed find him and came to round me up. The nurses asked us to wait in a very small private waiting area off to the side. I freaked! I had been asked to step into a small private waiting area the night they gathered the family together in the ER to tell us that mom had died. Peggy and Mary Jane quickly made sure the door was propped open and reassured me this was nothing like that. They eventually came and got us, and we got a peek at him. Oh, the tubes and contraptions! He was being kept sedated and on a breathing machine but he was doing okay. Now to find Dave.

Dave was doing okay, all things considered. He was receiving a fair amount of pain medication. Finally, our big day was over and everyone went home. I spent the night on a cot in a family area, exhausted but relieved it was over and both my boys were doing okay. That would prove to be short lived.

The next day, Dave began having trouble with the narcotics he was receiving. His blood pressure kept dropping to the point I had to call his parents to come and sit with him. They were planning on taking Nathan off the respirator, and I would need to be with him. Dave was bad enough at one point that I even had thoughts that somehow I'd had my wires crossed and it was him who might not make it. But once they cut out the narcotics and gave him straight Tylenol for pain, he quickly bounced back and was doing fine. Whew! Now we knew where Nathan got at least some of his intolerance for narcotics! We waited and waited, and they finally took Nathan off the respirator Saturday afternoon around 4 p.m. I now turn to my journal to tell the rest of the story:

> I laid down a little earlier to get a nap anticipating a sleepless night ahead. The nurse ran to get me and I got there just in time to see the tube being pulled. He was so puffy and his eyes swollen shut. He tried so hard to get them open but just couldn't. He was so groggy from the medication but unusually calm and even content under the circumstances. I remarked repeatedly how unusual this was for Nathan. He was usually cranky following surgery and typically had a croupy cough. To my amazement, he wasn't either. I remember feeling somewhat relieved yet somehow couldn't completely relax that we were out of the woods. Things were going too well. I tried to shake that uneasy feeling but it just wouldn't go away. Even though Nathan was weak and groggy, he managed to muster up the energy to talk. His words were very soft and mumbled but we eventually were able to understand most of what he was saying and his words became more and more clear and audible though weak. He managed to get us to turn on the TV, something he was very accustomed to in the hospital, and he also let us know he wanted the Cartoon Network. Then he asked for the remote. We laughed and obliged his requests. He weakly batted at the balloons with his hand and foot and even managed a smile and a chuckle. Despite all these things my gut said something was wrong. He eventually asked for his daddy and we made the arrangements for him to be brought up. What a wonderful and emotional reunion between father and son! A lot of the family was outside (the room) and took turns coming in and out and visiting with Nathan. He even teased with them, especially with Dave and his brother Mike. (Dave would put Mike's glasses on, and they would try to

get Nathan to believe Mike was Dave, unsuccessfully I might add!) *The visiting went on for several hours and it was obvious Nathan was getting tired and Dave needed to get back to his room.*

We all said our goodbyes. Dave's family left and went out to dinner to celebrate the events of the evening. Dave went back downstairs to get settled in for the night. I went for a sandwich as Nathan slipped back to sleep and stopped to check in on Dave before going back up to settle myself in for the night. They had a cot brought in for me (so I could sleep in the room with Nathan) *and I hadn't even gotten comfortable when Nathan woke up. He was croupy and struggling to breathe. His oxygen levels were falling. I held the blow-by near his face* (a tube that blew out oxygen). *That wasn't enough. I held the* (oxygen) *mask in front of his face—he didn't want it on. He weakly asked for water—which had become a "security blanket" for him—he was obviously uncomfortable. The situation got worse. They made the decision to put him back on the respirator for the night—something they assured me wasn't highly unusual. By morning, he should be fine and they could remove it again. They made preparations to put him back on the respirator. Nathan was more and more uncomfortable. They eventually sedated him. They gave me a worried look and asked me if I wanted to step out. I assured them I was fine and if I needed to I would do so quietly. I got up on my cot on my knees to be out of the way yet still be able to see what was going on. By this time the room was full of doctors and nurses. It was obvious the situation was getting serious. They were having trouble getting the tube down Nathan's throat. They were getting a little nervous. They were trying a little more frantically. Then his stomach sort of decompressed and they got the tube in but then couldn't get air forced in. They tried different settings on the machine. Then they tried another machine. More and more people had entered the room. Everyone knew exactly what their job was. You could tell they had done this type of thing many times before, only this time it was my son. I amazingly watched the whole battle with the tube and the machines with little or no emotion. My mind was desperately trying to make sense of the whole thing. I knew my son was in big trouble. But he had been in many tight places before and pulled through miraculously. Somehow I knew this was different.*

I began feeling called to leave. Absolutely not! There was no way I was going to leave my son here all alone and in such obvious trouble. But the call persisted and got stronger and stronger. I knew it was God calling me out of the room. I knew what He wanted. I didn't want to hear it. Somehow if I didn't hear it, it wasn't true. But I finally agreed with a very heavy heart. I don't know if anyone saw me when I left or not.

Now where? I first thought of going to Dave's room and grabbing my Bible but he had had such a rough few days I didn't want to wake him and worry him. Who knows? My overactive imagination and worry-wart nature could be way off base. Right?

I felt God calling me to the chapel. I again resisted not wanting to be alone with Him right now. I just knew what He was going to tell me. I just couldn't bear it! But that's eventually where I ended up. I sat for awhile then grabbed a Gideon Bible. I searched for the answers I so desperately needed to hear... the reassurance I so desperately needed that all was going to be all right. So many times before, I had searched the Bible for just that and God had so graciously provided it. But not this time. No matter what reference I looked up for "peace," "grace," "healing," "trust," etc., none of them told me things were going to be ok. They all reassured me of God's sovereignty...or of His grace in times of trouble...that He was in control...that He would be beside me...that He would provide me with all that I needed...not one word about Nathan being ok. I began crying out to

God. I begged, I bargained, I pleaded. "No, God!!! This can't be!!! Not my son!!! Not now!!! This surgery was supposed to make our lives somewhat normal for the first time since before Nathan was born. It was supposed to 'fix' our lives, Nathan's life, not tear it apart! What kind of testimony will this be of You? Let him live and people will certainly praise you for it! Please God!" I'm not sure how long I was down there in that chapel wrestling with God but by the time I left I knew Nathan was going to die. And I had to surrender myself and my son to God's will no matter how difficult and impossible it seemed to me. I had to give my son back to God. Oh, how my heart ached!!! The pain was so incredible I didn't know how I could live!!!

It was the longest and hardest walk back upstairs to the seventh floor. They made me wait in that dreaded little room. Once before I had waited in a dreaded little room when a doctor came in and told us that mom had died in a car accident. Now here I was once again in a little room waiting for them to come and tell me that my son was dead. I made them prop the door open with a trash can. I refused to be shut up all alone in that terrible little place. They came out and asked me if I had someone who could be with me. I said no and that I would be fine. Then they came back and said I needed to call someone and have them be with me. I called Dad. He said he'd be right there. It seemed like an eternity before he got there. They came back out again and said I needed to get my husband up there. Dad and I made phone calls to Peggy and Gordon and John Thomas. The word quickly spread even at that early hour of the morning—by now it was around 4 a.m. Things had changed so drastically from twelve hours ago.

Dave came up completely shocked and bewildered as to what could've happened. Friends and family slowly began to arrive to be with us, to encourage us even though most of them were as pitiful as we were.

14 Our Worst Nightmare

The docs came out and said that Nathan had had a massive heart attack. He had been without oxygen for some time. There was probable brain damage. His only chance was to be put on something called ECMO which was a life support system to give his body a rest. We gave permission to have it done even though chances were very slim. We once again wanted to give our son every opportunity to live that we possibly could. We called for Lynn to bring Ashley over. We felt she needed to be part of this too. She had shared in all of Nathan's battles and she needed to be there for this. I explained to her on the phone that Nathan was really sick and was probably going to be with Jesus and that she needed to come and be with us and see him if she wanted to. She came but decided not to go in. That was okay with us especially after we had seen him—we knew it was not a good idea for her to see her little brother like that. She clung to Lynn for the comfort and reassurance she needed. Dave and I were not able to give it to her ourselves.

After the procedure to hook Nathan up to the life support machine, Dave and I went in to see Nathan. He lay very quietly and completely still on top of a bed that had been elevated in order for them to work with him. He was still obviously full of extra fluid but the swelling had gone down somewhat and his face looked more like Nathan. But we both knew he wasn't there. Nathan was dead. There was something in his appearance—you just knew. My last hope was fading fast as I stood and looked at our baby boy. I stroked his fingers and his hair...our little boy was gone. Gone. I couldn't quite comprehend just what had happened in the last few hours. How could OUR little Nathan be lying here hooked up to a life support machine? What had gone wrong? "Oh God do something! Even now, even this is not out of your power to change things! Think of the testimony it would be!" I knew my last minute pleading was futile. God had made His decision. This was all part of His plan for Nathan and for us.

It was a long day as we waited to learn whether there was any brain activity or not. The first test said no. We waited for the second test. If it said no too, we would be faced with the decision as to whether or not to continue life support. The second test said no brain activity. We agreed to have him removed from the machine. Anyone who wanted to could go in and see Nathan. Then Dave and I went in to be with Nathan as they unhooked the machine. Nifty went in with us in case we needed him. (Nifty was there from the church filling in as Pastor Dan had left earlier for the Southern Baptist Convention.) *We stood by the bed and watched as the nurses clamped off the tubes. Blood was running from Nathan's nose. His body had gone through so much and was sort of breaking down from all the stuff they had done to him in the last few hours. It wouldn't stop no matter how much I wiped it. They finally stuffed it with cotton because it obviously bothered me. As soon as they cut the tubes, his lips began turning blue. Even though I believe Nathan had already died and left his body hours earlier, it was still very hard to stand there and watch your son being unhooked from a life support machine.* (Nathan was pronounced dead at 6:05 p.m., Sunday, June 7.) *They asked me if I wanted some of his hair. I said no. He had pooped under all the trauma and they changed his diaper. They taped off his tubes and got him cleaned up so I could hold him one last time. They got me a rocking chair and a pillow and gently laid him and his blanket on my lap on the pillow. He felt especially heavy with all the fluid he had on board. I remembered almost seven years ago sitting in a rocking chair just down the hall in the NICU and holding a tiny baby boy wrapped in a blanket and laying on a pillow. I remember turning my chair and facing the wall or window and crying because of what he had to face. He was so tiny and innocent. I remember wondering why it had to be that way. That seemed like another lifetime ago. Now I sat here holding my little baby boy and crying and wondering again why it had to be this way. I stroked his hands, his feet, his legs, his hair..."Oh, God why? Why?" My heart was completely broken in two. I had never in my life experienced such pain! Not even when mom died did I hurt so much as this. This was my child...my only son...gone...how could I go on? I finally gave up my little boy and went down the hall. What were we going to do now? I just wanted to get out of there...to go home...*

Nathan Still a Gift of God

Our Son's Funeral

Dave was released early from the hospital under the circumstances. Dave's dad arranged to take us home in Dave's Grandma's car because of the smooth ride for Dave's sake.

We went to Dave's parents' house. Dave needed a regular bed to sleep in, there was no way he would be able to sleep in our water bed. We were exhausted of course, but even then it was a very restless night.

The next morning I still had this overwhelming need to be home. So home we went. We made arrangements for a hospital bed to be brought to the house for Dave. We began to be engulfed by wave after wave of family and friends. It was amazing the love and support and provision that so many made for us. Whatever was needed, it somehow appeared, down to extra refrigerators for all the food. Our friend Charles Reynolds of the Reynolds Funeral Home was an absolute God-send. He took care of all the arrangements without us even having to leave the house. Aunt Tammy did the unthinkable as she went shopping for clothes for Nathan to be buried in and met all our requests, down to finding a cartoon tie. (Dave had quite a collection of ties with various cartoon characters that he wore for work. As a result Nathan had developed quite the love of ties and bowties himself wanting to be like his daddy. Naturally he had to be buried in one!) I'll never know how difficult that task was for her as she may never know how much that meant for her to do that for us.

We finally went to the funeral home to see Nathan—it had taken several days for them to do the autopsy and release the body. The doctors at U.Va. had requested the autopsy in hopes it would reveal what went wrong and perhaps help someone in the future. Of course we agreed. We were saddened that none of his organs could be donated because of the breakdown that had occurred throughout his body. The only thing that was salvageable was his corneas. Those big, beautiful but mischievous brown eyes! Almost the first thing after we arrived, some little old lady that I didn't even know came up and stood beside me. She put her arm around me and said something about God needing another little angel in Heaven. It was all I could do not to lay her out in the floor I was so mad! And what was she doing there anyway? I walked away before I hurt her.

We stood before the casket, and the first thing I noticed was that his hair was too neat! Strange what you think of at times like these! So we messed up his hair. It didn't seem possible our little boy was laying there in a casket. This couldn't be happening. But there he was. His skin was so cold and so hard. That night we had family night in the same room where mom had been, the "blue room." Nathan had been in that same room not that long ago when someone had died and he asked where Jesus was. I didn't understand what he was saying at first, and he was obviously getting frustrated with me. Then I figured it out. Nathan had heard enough times that when someone died they went to be with Jesus. So here he was in the room with someone who had died, and if you die you go to be with Jesus, then Jesus must be in the house! So naturally, he wanted to see Jesus! Precious! Try explaining to a five-year-old why he couldn't see Jesus!

On family night, we received family and friends for hours. Despite still recovering from major surgery, Dave made it through the night rather well. Danny, our youth pastor, personally made sure Dave was as comfortable as possible for the long evening with drinks, snacks, and an occasional pat on the back.

Nathan died on Sunday and we finally buried him on Thursday. Pastor Dan had returned early from the convention to be there for us and, of course, to preach the funeral. The service was lovely—if your son's funeral can be so. My brother sang "Awesome God" by Rich Mullins,

15 Our Son's Funeral

Nathan's favorite. When Nathan would hear it on the radio, he would belt out the words along with it. I especially remember him doing this in the car as I would be driving. We had also asked that the gospel be presented. It was, and several made professions of faith. But perhaps the thing that stood out most was all the people. There were cars and people everywhere. Hundreds of people came to love on us and support us during the most difficult time of our lives. Perhaps the neatest thing to see was the fire engine. Nathan loved fire trucks and had even taken a ride in our local volunteer station's new engine. And there it sat, right in front of the church! Once the service was over then came the hardest, most difficult part of all—walking behind the casket as it is slowly rolled down the center aisle of the church. A painfully long and difficult walk.

Then, the long ride to the cemetery. Along the way, just at the city limits stood two young boys, perhaps young teens, along side their bikes. They had stopped and were saluting as the funeral procession drove past. It's always the small things that touch you so much. After they had placed Nathan in the ground and as the crowd was breaking up to head back home, the fire engine rode past and blasted its siren. A fitting salute to our little firefighter!

We came back to the house for a meal. A friend from church, had made arrangements and personally handled getting a large event tent put up in the yard for everyone to have a meal with us. Another friend had come and planted flowers around the house so it would look nice for the afternoon. So many people, so many blessings I could never remember them all. It was interesting that somewhere during the course of the afternoon I lost my angel pin that Peggy had given me. I know it sounds silly, but in a way those "angels on my shoulders" were no longer needed, and as much as I hated to lose that pin, it was rather symbolic that it was lost on that day.

Nathan Still a Gift of God

Life Goes On

Dave's brother Steven and Audra went ahead with their wedding scheduled for that weekend. There was no reason to postpone their big day. Dave and I attended. It was the first of many occasions where we simply went through the motions doing what we "knew" to do because we had no clue what we were "supposed" to do, if you know what I mean. Dave and I both managed to stay numb until they presented us with a rose in honor of Nathan as part of the ceremony. We were so touched by their thoughtfulness.

After the funeral, Dave's surgery site simply would not heal and instead began to drain. That led to a number of trips back and forth to the doctor to correct the problem, and eventually took cauterizing it with silver nitrate to get it to stop draining. Then at the end of June, I packed up all the medical stuff from the house and made the trip to U.Va. to return it all. Strange how hard it was to return things that had been such a burden and trial. It felt like the end of something, the closing of a big part of our life. It was a very sad thing and left me with such a feeling of "now what?" This was all I had known for so long.

I composed a note and presented it to the doctors and nurses of U.Va. in the weeks following Nathan's death:

> *About seven years ago, we gave birth to a beautiful baby boy. Although by the world's standards, he was not "perfect," we believed Nathan was a true gift from God and without a doubt was meant to be. As you know, Nathan was a rather medically involved little boy having his first surgery before he was even born. The medical world was uncharted territory for us, and we were scared, nervous, intimidated, and at times, completely overwhelmed with his medical needs. But along with our medically needy child, God blessed us with the absolute best medical facility and*

> some of the most incredible doctors, nurses and staff the medical field has to offer!!! You were there with us every step of the way...from the day Nathan came screaming into this world until the day he silently slipped away. There are no words to express to each of you how grateful we are for all you have done for our family and for Nathan over the past seven years. You not only provided us with your topnotch medical skill, but also befriended our entire family. Nathan is a prime example that life is filled with all sorts of trials, adversities and pain. Nathan also showed us that life is what you make it. Nathan made the most of his short, challenged life and lived it to the fullest. We thank God for giving us Nathan and all the joy he brought to our lives. We thank God for giving us each of you to make our time with Nathan the best that it could be.

God began to speak to me through His Word again. On July 5, God gave me Psalm 125:1-2: [1]*Those who trust in the Lord are like Mount Zion, which cannot be shaken but endures forever. [2]As the mountains surround Jerusalem, so the Lord surrounds his people both now and forevermore.* He also gave me Psalm 126:5-6: [5]*Those who sow in tears will reap with songs of joy. [3]He who goes out weeping, carrying seed to sow, will return with songs of joy, carrying sheaves with him.*

Then began quite a bit of journaling from the heart of a grieving mother:

> *Today is Tuesday, July 7, 1998. Exactly one month ago today Nathan died. I'm not even sure at this point I completely understand exactly what that statement means....Nathan died.....Nathan is dead......Nathan is gone. For the past month, I've struggled with this statement....this fact. No matter how hard I try, I don't seem to quite have the mental capacity to process this information and the tremendous impact it has and will have on my (our) life (lives). It's as if parts of my*

16 Life Goes On

brain have shut down and I am unable to access these areas in order to come to terms with "Nathan died."

On July 12, we were asked to come to the Wilson Fire Station, our local volunteer station, where we were presented with a plaque that read: *Presented Posthumously to Nathan Sours as Honorary Member Wilson Volunteer Fire Company 19.* Oh, how Nathan would have loved that!

On July 26, I was reading Psalm 138, which speaks of praising the Lord. I wasn't there! I couldn't conceive of even the possibility at this point, if ever (Appendix, 3). And then on that same day, I stumbled across a verse I had never taken notice of before. I've jokingly said that God added it in just for me at this time of my life when I needed it most. Psalm 139:16: *Your eyes saw my unformed body. All the days ordained for me were written in your book before one of them came to be.* Nathan's days were ordained by God. Though they were short in my eyes, they were exactly what they were supposed to be in God's plan. Hard to swallow, but somehow reassuring that even the short days Nathan was allowed here on earth, he had accomplished God's purpose for his life and was done.

On July 27, my identifying with the psalmist began in a whole new way. Psalm 144:4 spoke of what I was dealing with: *Man is like a breath; his days are like a fleeting shadow.* Psalm 142 was one of those that seemed to speak for me:

> [1]*I cry aloud to the Lord; I lift up my voice to the Lord for mercy.* [2]*I pour out my complaint before him; before him I tell my trouble.* [3]*When my spirit grows faint within me, it is you who knows my way. In the path where I walk men have hidden a snare for me.* [4]*Look to my right and see; no one is concerned for me. I have no refuge; no one cares for my life.* [5]*I cry to you, O Lord; I say, "You are my refuge, my portion in the land of the living."* [6]*Listen to my cry, for I am in desperate need; rescue me from those who pursue*

me, for they are too strong for me. ⁷*Set me free from my prison, that I may praise your name. Then the righteous will gather about me because of your goodness to me.*

I was also reminded that "the Lord lifts up all who are bowed down"[109] and that He understands.[110] But the words of Psalm 143:4 were so close to my own heart: *My spirit grows faint within me; my heart within me is dismayed.*

Toward the end of July, we decided to get away for awhile. Dave especially seemed to want that. We decided to go camping somewhere Nathan had never been. We chose Myrtle Beach. I silently cried most of the way there. It seemed so strange, even wrong, to be going camping without Nathan. It was a very subdued camping trip. We went through the motions but had little, if any, heart to put into anything. Dave would spend his nights alone out on the beach fishing. I would spend much of my time alone wrestling with our new reality. Ashley was obviously unsure of what to do with her parents. To make matters worse, there seemed to be little boys everywhere we turned! One night I decided to go to the laundry room to wash some clothes thinking it would be a safe place to be alone. WRONG! There was a group of younger boys playing in and around the building the whole time I was there. I was trapped! All in all, I guess it was a good thing to get away but rather than leaving anything behind, we took it all with us. There was no escaping the death, loss, and absence of our little Nathan.

My journal entry on August 6:

> *Today is Thursday, August 6, 1998. Tomorrow marks the two month anniversary of my son's death. At the present, I'm home alone....Dave went fishing and Ashley's at her cousin Keri's house. Being home alone is very tough these days. It's so very, very quiet! Too quiet! A disturbing quiet. A quiet that only serves as a big gigantic reminder that Nathan is not here......*

> will not ever be here.....ever. I'm so used to the noise of life with Nathan. His laughter, his giggles, his little feet running at an unsteady pace through the house usually followed by a loud "thud" as he would trip and fall to the floor or into a nearby wall, his yelling Mom! or Mommy!, toys being dumped from a basket or falling from shelves with a loud crash, the variety of noises he produced with all those loud boy toys, the "loving" exchanges between Nathan and his sister, my voice echoing through the house exasperated with his latest escapade. Now.....SILENCE!!! I'm so used to functioning under stress and chaos. Now I find it difficult to focus....remain on task....to think....it's just too quiet.

On August 13, I attended a local grief group. While it was good to be with others who could understand, I felt strangely out of place. It just didn't fit for some reason.

On August 23, God spoke to me through Jeremiah where He is telling Israel to settle down and get used to their new home in captivity because they are going to be here awhile.[111] I felt like that was His message to me in my grief. My pain and loss obviously weren't going anywhere anytime soon. I was going to be here awhile.

Nathan Still a Gift of God

Back to School

Summer came to an end all too soon. Like it or not, it was time for Ashley to go back to school and for me to go back to work. Once again, I was faced with what seemed an impossible task.

> Today is Monday, August 24, 1998. Today is the first day of school. It would have been Nathan's first day in first grade. He would have been so excited!! By today, he would have gone through his school supplies at least fifty times checking each one out, asking if he could use the markers and the paper and the notebooks. He would have asked a thousand questions about what first grade would be like. Asked at least that many times who his teacher was....where his class was....would so-and-so be in his class. This morning would have been full of excitement as he got dressed and all ready for his first big day! He would have had to have just the right outfit and especially the right shoes (he loved shoes!) He would have had to gather up all the school supplies that he would have probably dumped again at the last minute to give them one last going over. The house would have been filled with his giggles and probably my voice encouraging him to hurry up or we'd be late and using all sorts of reminders that he needed to be on time so he wouldn't miss anything or maybe if we'd hurry he could play in my room for awhile before he went to his new class. We probably would've made three or four trips back into the house in order to make sure we had everything. There would've probably been a spat or two between brother and sister as they undoubtedly would've rubbed each other the wrong way in one aspect or another. We would've hurried on down the road with reminders to be a good listener, use good manners, be nice to your teacher and friends, etc. Once we got to school there probably would've been a scolding because Nathan

would've dumped all his stuff out of his book bag AGAIN! to take one more look! Then the monumental task of getting everyone and everything across the parking lot without getting hit or dropping something and then (making our way) down the sidewalk. Maybe if we were lucky there would've been time in my room to play for a few minutes while I caught my breath from the morning's frantic effort to get to school on time. Then I would've walked my son to his new room and gotten a big hug and a wet kiss and big smile and heard the words "I love you!"

    That's the way the day should've been. The way I wish with all my heart it had been. But it wasn't. There was no frantic chaotic morning getting ready for school. All was too calm. We weren't hurried. We weren't late. There were no school supplies to repack for the thousandth time. There were no hugs and kisses from my little boy as he entered first grade. There was no one to hurry down the sidewalk before the bell rang. There was no mischievous little grin and a big wave to greet me as I entered the cafeteria for lunch. No little fellow to tell me how his first day of first grade was and no conference with a teacher to find out the real truth! Nathan's not here. School went on as usual. Without Nathan. It seems so unfair. He was going to have such a good year. He had made so much progress in kindergarten. We had such high hopes for first grade. Life was going to be so much better after transplant.

    I can't tell anyone exactly how I feel. How much I hurt. How empty my life is. How much I miss my Nathan. How cheated I feel. How unfair life is. How there seems no end to the pain and the emptiness and the loneliness.....ever. I feel I'm fighting a losing battle. I feel I'm slipping closer and closer into a bottomless pit. There's nothing I can do to stop it. I'm trying so desperately to be wife and mom at the very least, and even in those areas I feel I'm losing ground. Ashley is starting to show more and more signs of grieving

17 Back to School

> *and coming to some sort of terms with the death of Nathan. I'm not sure how or what to do to help her except to be there to listen and talk and be aware of what's going on. I don't feel I'm on top of things where she's concerned though. And with Dave....I feel there are walls springing up between us. More and more all the time. He seems to have so much anger. And I seem to be the outlet lots of time. Little things are big deals to him right now. And I don't have the desire or the energy to help him work this out. We don't talk very much except surface things. Rarely mention Nathan except briefly and something light and non-threatening. It's becoming more and more clear why statistics show eighty percent of marriages fail following the death of a child. We both know we've lost so much and neither of us wants to lose even more but at the same time neither one of us has it in us to put a lot of effort into our relationship. Men and women grieve differently. Dave and I grieve differently and handle things differently. It's a vicious thing—grief. We do have lots of caring and loving people who are there for us....praying for us....encouraging us. But it's still tough!*

In the first few days back at school, it was obvious there was a pink elephant in the room, so I wrote a letter to the school staff to try and ease that a bit:

A message to our Ladd family as I returned back to work:

> *In September 1994, a very hesitant and tearful "young" mother brought her two children to Ladd Elementary on the first day of school. Ashley had just turned 5 and had a very severe case of "mommy-itis" and cried for the first 6-8 weeks of kindergarten. Nathan, only 2 ½ years old, was entering the Early Childhood class. He had been very medically involved all his life and could barely walk or talk. As the*

Nathan Still a Gift of God

commercial goes..."We've come a long way, baby!" Ashley is in the fourth grade now and is becoming a lovely young lady (most of the time!). As for Nathan, in no time at all, our quiet and immobile little boy wouldn't sit down or shut up! And I was so thrilled with Ladd and especially the Early Childhood program. I soon became the aide in Nathan's classroom. From the very beginning, we were impressed not only with the quality of education but especially with the people at Ladd. We felt very fortunate to have our children attend such a fine school! During our days at Ladd, Nathan won the hearts of most everyone he met. He had a wonderful little smile that he got a lot of mileage out of and when that didn't work he'd throw in a hug and a "I wub you!" Only his mother and his teacher could resist and some days even THEY fell victim to his charm!!! Nathan's health continued to deteriorate and we soon found ourselves gearing up for a kidney transplant. However, we found we were not facing transplant alone. We had our Ladd family with us every step of the way. And when the unthinkable happened and Nathan died as a result of complications from transplant, you continued to be there for us with an amazing display of love and support that was absolutely incredible!!! We could never thank each of you enough for all the acts of kindness you've shown to our family...the notes and cards, the flowers and plants, your donations to the various organizations in honor of Nathan, the food, the calls, the visits, and the list goes on and on!!! There are simply no words to express how much we appreciate everything you've done to support and encourage our family in the death of Nathan. We offer you only a humble "thank you!" It was a very tough decision to come back to work at Ladd. No matter where I turn I'm reminded of Nathan and the fact he's not here. But I'm also reminded on a daily basis of how blessed I am to be a part of such a loving and supportive work environment. And please know it's

17 Back to School

okay to talk about Nathan...to mention his name...to remember him. Thoughts of Nathan fill my mind and heart every day...every hour. When you mention him I may cry (actually, that's a very real possibility at this point!) but it's okay. It's all part of the healing process and it means so much to know that he was special to all of you as well. We still have a long road ahead of us as we face life without Nathan. I hang on (by a very thin thread some days!) to God's promises and His strength and with the love and support of friends like you we will find our way through the pain and devastation of losing Nathan.

There would continue to be challenges and adjustments for all of us throughout the course of the school year, but the continued love and support of our school family got us through.

Nathan Still a Gift of God

Journey Into Grief

I continued to meet with Nifty. A number of people thought I needed to do that. Because I had a difficult time communicating my thoughts and feelings with Dave, Nifty suggested I write Dave a letter in order to give him some insight as to what was going on with me. I did and it actually opened the door for a conversation or two. Our relationship was definitely strained. Some days it bothered me more than others. Most days I did not have the energy to even care.

On September 13, I read about the dry bones coming to life in Ezekiel.[112] I felt like God was suggesting I might actually live again but I didn't see how that would ever be possible. God spoke to me again on the twenty-sixth, this time having the audacity to speak of joy! John 15:11: *I have told you this so that my joy may be in you and that your joy may be complete.* The footnote even suggested I could have joy in the midst of my grief!

> *When things are going well we feel elated. When hardships come we sink into depression. But true joy transcends the rolling waves of circumstance. Joy comes from a consistent relationship with Jesus Christ. When our lives are intertwined with his he will help us walk through adversity without sinking into debilitating lows and manage prosperity without moving into deceptive highs. The joy of living with Jesus Christ daily will keep us levelheaded no matter how high or low our circumstances.*[113]

God also gave me Lamentations 3:31-32: *[31]For men are not cast off by the Lord forever. [32]Though he brings grief, he will show compassion, so great is his unfailing love.*

We got word that the autopsy report was in and so we set up a meeting to discuss it with Nurse Fern on October 1. I desperately needed to know the results of the autopsy hoping it would provide some insight into Nathan's death. Maybe then, I would have some sort of closure. Dave on the other hand did not feel a need to be part of that meeting and had actually planned to go golfing that afternoon. Personally, I felt it was yet another attempt to avoid the issue. I was really hurt that he could not see I needed him there for me but my pride would not allow me to ask him to come. But Pastor Dan discovered Dave was not planning on going with me and he called Dave and told him though he may not feel he needed to be there for himself, he needed to be there for me. Somewhat reluctantly Dave cancelled his plans and went to the meeting with me.

The three of us met in a little conference room. I can't quite explain what it feels like to be sitting around a table discussing your son's autopsy results. Dave was quiet and unemotional for the most part during the entire meeting. I, on the other hand, was my usual emotional self and full of questions. I wanted some explanation for Nathan's unexpected death. I wanted at least one answer to the million times I had asked, "Why?!" I don't know what I thought the knowledge would bring me but I wanted to make some sense of his senseless death. Unfortunately I would leave with most of the same questions I came in with.

The official cause of death was a "massive acute myocardial infarction due to a hypotensive event of unknown etiology." In other words, Nathan died of a massive heart attack, cause unknown. The report showed extensive damage to most of his vital organs which the renal doctors believed was a result of being on ECMO life support for so long because it does not oxygenate the body efficiently. They also discovered a blood clot although they did not feel that contributed to his death. We didn't get a clear picture as to the cause of Nathan's death but we did have a much better understanding of what went on during those dreaded twenty-four hours or so. He was taken off the respirator around 3:30-4 p.m. on Saturday afternoon. Dave came up around 6:30pm. Nathan was given the anti-rejection medicine around 8:30 p.m. He started having trouble breathing around 10 p.m. and his oxygen levels dropped and his blood pressure went up. At 11:45 p.m. they put him back on the respirator. Around 1 a.m., his oxygen levels dropped. At 2 a.m. they had to do a few compressions but he came back. Then around 3:45 a.m. Nathan coded having a massive heart attack. He was given epinephrine and compressions were started at 4:21 and continued until he was placed on ECMO (life support at 7 a.m. His pupils were not reactive when checked at 8:10 a.m.

The report itself was unable to explain to us the cause of death. Most likely there were a number of things that contributed. Nathan had a history of having a very low tolerance for sedation and pain medication. Then, the transplant surgery had taken much longer than expected and he was kept sedated afterward because of being intubated. I personally believe the drugs had built up in his body to the point that when his lungs began filling with fluid, his heart and body could not meet the demand and he ended up having a heart attack. We left the hospital with more questions than what we came in with: what could have been done differently? Did I explain his sensitivity to drugs well enough? Did they listen? Was enough done to prevent the fluid build up in his lungs? Our questions would probably never be answered, at least not in this life time but they were questions I was sure would continue to haunt me for the rest of my life.

I had visited several grief support groups in and around the area. Somehow I just couldn't find one that fit for me although each one seemed to be doing a tremendous job for those in attendance. We had had several deaths in our church family over the last several months, so I approached Nifty and suggested (actually was willing to beg!) that he start one. Surprisingly, he didn't put up much resistance to the idea and was actually all for it, IF I would help him. I had no choice but to agree because I was in desperate need of "something," hoping this group might just be the thing. So on Monday, October 5, we held the first meeting of the WHBC Grief Education and Support Group. We had seven or eight of us who began a journey of a lifetime together.

On October 13, God gave me some profound words from Ecclesiastes 8:17:

> *Then I saw all that God has done. No one can comprehend what goes on under the sun. Despite all his efforts to search it out, man cannot discover its meaning. Even if a wise man claims he knows, he cannot really comprehend it.*

Even though I would never fully understand why Nathan had to die so young, I could trust that God was still in control.

My journaling continued:

> *Today is Saturday, November 7. Nathan died five months ago today. This may sound weird but at times it seems harder to remember exactly what it was like before he died.....as if my mind struggles with the reality of Nathan's existence. It's hard to explain. The one true evidence of his existence is the hole his death has left in my life, my heart, my very soul. I look at the many pictures of Nathan around the house and try to recapture him and life at that moment. It's as if I'm afraid I'm going to forget the many, many memories I have of him.....the way he smiled, the way he walked, the way he laughed, his cry, his chubby little fingers, his medicine stained teeth, the mischievous gleam in his eye, his humor, his manipulative ways, the way he ate, how he loved to check things out, take things apart (and seldom put them back together again!), and even the times he was sick, getting up in the middle of the night so many, many times, croup, shots, getting him to take his "yucky" medicine, reading to him........my heart aches for those days that will be no more! Life*

is so very empty without him! In everything I've read (and that's a lot!), I'm assured by many who have lost children themselves that the journey through grief will one day get easier. One day the ache will go away and I'll be able to remember the days with Nathan with a smile and maybe an occasional tear but it <u>will</u> get easier. I also have the assurance from God & His Word that I am just passing <u>through</u> the valley of the shadow of death. My head knows these things but the ache in my heart causes me to doubt those truths some days....well, actually most days!

God at Work

My marriage wasn't the only relationship that was suffering. I also had a real attitude with God. Back in the spring, I felt God calling me to do a ladies retreat. I tried to get out of it then thinking the upcoming transplant was reason enough for someone else to do it. I even went to Pastor Dan hoping he would agree with me and thinking I would certainly get a little sympathy from the pastor under the circumstances. Fat chance! He said I had better obey God. Reluctantly, I worked with Nifty and put together the retreat. It quickly became obvious as we worked on it that God was preparing to do a great work through retreat. But that was before transplant. That was before my world literally fell apart. I had a real issue with God about the whole thing. He knew even before He called me to do the retreat that Nathan was going to die and He called me anyway! God knew as we were putting the material together what I would be facing when it came time to pull it off. And He had me do it anyway! And here I was an absolute mess unable to organize a complete thought much less a ladies retreat. I could not even balance my checkbook for goodness sakes! Yeah, I had quite a chip on my shoulder as I moved ahead in obedience.

I would later repent of my attitude with God about the retreat. It was without a doubt the most amazing weekend ever! God did an incredible work in the lives of the ladies who were in attendance. Everyone felt His presence in such a powerful and personal way. I was unable to do anything. I was completely empty. But in my weakness, He was my strength. He did it all! I was just obedient. He selected the speakers and other than to come together and pray for the retreat, we did not have a single planning session. The speakers put together their own sessions for the retreat. We could have met and planned for months and still not have been able to do what God did through the course of the weekend! Through each speaker, He wove together a weekend theme of being rooted in Him, bearing fruit, trimming out sin and hurts, and being watered by His Word.

I also had to repent of my "alright, I'll do it but I'm not working on me" attitude. I managed to keep my walls of resistance up until Saturday afternoon during our quite time alone with God. Boy, He tore those walls down and gave me such a keen sense of His presence! My prayer had always been for God to be glorified in Nathan's life and now in his death. God showed me I could not expect Nathan's life and death to impact other people if I did not first let it impact me. Up to that point, even though I had been going to counseling and attending a support group, I had a great fear of experiencing the immense pain of losing Nathan. I had a great fear of going back to the pit of depression not knowing how far down I'd go or how long I would be there or if I would ever come back. So I had made the choice to avoid as much of the grief process as possible because it was all I could do to function. But God was making it pretty clear that I was going to have to deal with Nathan's death for my own well being but also if I could ever expect Him to use it for His glory. I was still afraid but somehow I had the assurance I would not be making that journey alone. God would be with me and would bring me out the other side.

I had been experiencing an unusual turmoil inside. It felt like a searching, a longing, an internal gnawing. I spent some time fasting, praying, and seeking God that He might reveal to me what it was all about. On November 12th in my quiet time with Him He did just that: speak! First through the profile on Isaiah:

> Isaiah may have been established as a scribe. It was a respectable career, but God had other plans for his servant. Isaiah's account of God's call leaves little doubt about what motivated the prophet for the next half century. His vision

of God was unforgettable…eventually some would listen. God compared his people to a tree that would have to be cut down so that a new tree could grow from the old stump. We also gain the hope of knowing that God is active in all of history, including our own.[114]

Next God spoke to me from Isaiah 6:8: *Then I heard the voice of the Lord saying, "Whom shall I send? And who will go for us?" And I said, "Here am I. Send me!"* The footnote added:

No matter how difficult his task would be, he said, "Here am I. Send me!" The painful cleansing process was necessary before Isaiah could fulfill the task to which God was calling him. Before we accept God's call to speak for him to those around us, we must be cleansed as Isaiah was, confessing our sins and submitting to God's control. Letting God purify us may be painful, but we must be purified so that we can truly represent God, who is pure and holy. The more clearly Isaiah saw God, the more aware Isaiah became of his own powerlessness and inadequacy to do anything of lasting value without God. But he was willing to be God's spokesman. When God calls, will you also say, "Here am I. Send me!"?[115]

God showed me three things in my time with him that day. First, He reminded me I had a good job as an instructional aide. The pay wasn't the greatest but I knew that was where God had placed me. However, God had something else for me now but I would have to be patient and willing to allow Him to guide me to whatever that may be. Second, I felt God reinforcing the idea that the journaling I had done since I was pregnant with Nathan would one day be in print. That would definitely have to be a God-thing! And finally and perhaps most importantly at this point in my life, I felt God telling me though I felt like I was cut down to a pitiful ol' stump with Nathan's death, He was going to grow me into a new tree! I didn't know how long it would take or what kind but one day I would be a new tree.

My brother Dave asked me if I'd like to go with him to a local prison and share my testimony as part of the on-going ministry he was involved with there. If you remember, I had made a promise to God when I was pregnant with Nathan that if He let Nathan live, I would never turn down an opportunity to share what He had done for us. I agreed although my testimony was now one of what God was doing for us in Nathan's death not life. I prayed and asked God specifically what He would have me share with the men there and one morning at 4 a.m. God answered, "Give them hope and encouragement." He also gave me some scriptures to share with them from Corinthians where Paul talks about "being hard pressed on every side and crushed but not broken." He also gave me a passage from Isaiah where it says "when you pass through the waters, they will not over take you." And finally, He wanted me to talk about giving control over to God not just in my own life but with Nathan as well.

It was an incredible evening. The men were very warm and inviting and came up afterward and shared their own stories of not having seen their children in years or stories of how they were watching their children choose wrong paths for themselves or stories of loved ones who had died. They thanked me for reminding them God is in control and will bring them through. It was an interesting experience to say the least and maybe one I would not have chosen for myself but it was exactly where I needed to be.

My next journal entry brought my focus back to the task at hand—grief:

> *Today is Monday, November 16. My heart, mind, and soul are so full.....so overwhelmed with this thing called "grief." It affects every aspect of my life. I feel so very alone in my grief. Even Dave and I can't connect*

in our grief and we've both lost the same son. I don't feel as if there's anyone there just for me. Someone who knows me, understands what I'm feeling and how I'm struggling. Someone to listen without passing judgment as to how I "should" be doing or feeling. I'd love to be able to crawl up on Mom's lap and have her rock me and make it all go away. (Even as an adult, I'd still sit on my mama's lap and chat. I was so homesick on my honeymoon, the first thing I did when we got back was go home and have my mama rock me!) But I don't feel like I have anyone except God and sometimes even He seems so far away.

It's very interesting how God works. I've just come from a grief support meeting at our church. A support group that is somewhat a result of Nathan's death. I mean who would have ever thought that some day I'd be co-leading a grief support group? Certainly not me! I wish with all my heart the events that led to this group coming into being had never happened. But I can't help coming away with a warm feeling knowing that even in the terrible loss of my son something good has come about as a result of his death. We have a group of about twelve or so that meet faithfully each week to share and comfort one another. We also are learning about this journey we are all on through grief. We know we're going to make it because we share a common belief that God is with us every step of the way! It's a long hard journey with Him; I can't imagine what it'd be without Him!

There was an unexpected blessing of the grief group. I had needed to connect with another mother who had experienced the loss of a child. I somehow ended up with a telephone number that I called and arranged to meet with a lady named Barb whose four-year-old daughter, Stephanie, had died a little over a year prior to Nathan. Barb and I instantly "clicked" and she began attending our grief support group. Barb also had a daughter the same age as Ashley named Jenna. Every Monday night, Barb and I would each go through the drive-thru (usually Taco Bell), pick up dinner for our daughters and meet at the church. While the adults had our grief meeting, Ashley and Jenna would have dinner and spend time together. They didn't necessarily sit around and talk about how they each felt, but they were having their own version of a grief support group all the same. Sometimes their "grief meeting" included roller blading through the church basement! As God would have it, Ashley and Jenna ended up at the same school in sixth grade, played volleyball together through high school, and are friends to this day although life has taken them in different directions. God was not only looking out for me, but He was taking care of Ashley at a time when I wasn't even able to take care of myself.

The First Thanksgiving

I went shopping for a weekend at an outlet mall with some of the teachers from Ladd. As far as shopping goes, it was one of the most productive shopping excursions I believe I had ever had. I managed to almost finish my Christmas shopping as well as buy birthday gifts for the upcoming year! But the more tired I became, the less energy I had for "keeping it together." I began to see all the small children, especially the little boys, running around the stores looking at all the neat boy-toys that were out. Some of them were naturally getting into trouble. I even saw one little boy who had hearing aids. It became increasingly difficult to fight back the tears. I would have given anything to be shopping for or even with Nathan, as difficult a task as that could be sometimes! Nathan absolutely loved Christmas and his birthday. The look of joy and excitement on his face as he would open up his presents was absolutely priceless! And one we would never enjoy again. I sat looking at all that was going on around me and wondered how on earth we would ever make it through the holiday season without him!

The first of my holiday journal entries written Thanksgiving morning:

> *Today is Thanksgiving. A day to count your blessings. To give thanks. I'll be the first to admit that I have a lot to be thankful for. I have wonderful husband even though lately we seem rather distant. I have a lovely daughter Ashley who is bright and an all-around delightful little girl who up to this point has been rather low maintenance. I have a lovely little house. Though nothing fancy it's "home" and my place of refuge. Plenty of food, clothes and so many material things many of which are extras God has blessed us with in addition to our needs being met. We all have health. We have a number of family and friends. And the list goes on. Despite a very long list of blessings*

all of which I'm very thankful for, I still am having a hard time having a thankful attitude. It's impossible for me to muster up that deep down warm fuzzy feeling of true thankfulness and excitement as today marks the beginning of the holiday season. Instead, I find myself overcome with such an extreme emptiness and loneliness. There are no words to describe how I'm feeling inside. My heart aches and longs for Nathan to be here with us. Driving me crazy no doubt! Even in the chaos of life with Nathan and all the demands he put on me (us) life was good. Life was full. He had such a spark to add to any occasion. A spark that no one can match. How I long to hold him...to hug him....to have one of his big, fat wet kisses.....to hear "I wub you!" I even miss those trying days where it was a battle of the wills! I never thought I'd say that! But those days, both good and bad, are gone forever! And I'm left with an ache in my heart that won't go away.

We somehow managed to get through the first of the holiday season and despite my thankless heart, I had to admit it wasn't as bad as I had anticipated. Actually the anticipation of Thanksgiving day was worse than the actual day itself. I did have quite a meltdown Thursday afternoon when I had some unexpected time alone. I just cried and cried as I remembered last Thanksgiving with Nathan. Now, the house just screamed silence without him running about in excitement because of all the festivities surrounding the holiday season. He could eat his weight in stuffing, turkey, and green beans! Most of the time we had to monitor what Nathan ate but holidays were an exception and he took full advantage! It just didn't seem possible we were facing the holiday season without him, without the one who perhaps enjoyed it the most. But we were and, oh, how it hurt. It felt so empty, so unfair, and I cried! And I fully anticipated crying right through the upcoming days and weeks of holiday cheer! Bah! Humbug!

It was part of our annual family tradition to go to the local Christmas parade. It was certainly one tradition that I could have skipped but Ashley was insistent, so we went. I felt so torn trying to do for the child who still lives yet dying inside the whole while for the child that was dead. As we sat on the curb waiting for the parade to begin, I looked around at all the families. There were small children everywhere running, squealing, giggling, laughing, talking a mile a minute with all the excitement—it cut like a knife. Especially seeing all the little boys who seemed to follow me everywhere I went these days. Of course, I couldn't help but remember the last parade we went to and Nathan's excitement especially over the fire trucks and their loud sirens. Thankfully the parade started and I hoped to lose myself in the activity and be able to turn the memories and the emotions off for awhile. Not a chance. There were fire trucks, lots of fire trucks with sirens blaring. And more fire trucks and with each came more knives to the heart. Why did everything have to be such a blatant reminder that Nathan is not here with us enjoying life as only he could?! Even if I did manage to enjoy a moment, maybe even laugh a little bit, the harsh reality of Nathan's absence came back and slapped me in the face time and time again.

Nathan Still a Gift of God

The First Birthday

I hardly caught my breath from Thanksgiving before Nathan's birthday hit me the following Wednesday. Andrea had arranged a sub for me so I could have the day off. I got Dave off to work and Ashley off to school and there I was with no plan for the day other than to spend it in my pajamas and cry. I felt oddly uncomfortable not quite knowing what to do with myself so I started tidying up the house. I realized I was avoiding the inevitable so I got out the photo albums and proceeded to step back in time through all the events that composed our life with Nathan. Life was always full with Nathan. I don't think there was a single picture of him without that prize winning crooked smile of his that everyone so vividly remembers. After looking through the albums, I then added the pictures we had taken on the day before we went into the hospital, our last day together as a family. In those pictures were ones of Ashley and Nathan with their new kittens "Precious" and "Batman" (Can you guess which one belonged to whom?). There were pictures of Ashley and Nathan playing on the equipment and the "twisty slide" as Nathan referred to it. Others showed them feeding the ducks. The pictures brought back such good memories, treasured memories, and now memories were all we had left of the little boy in those pictures.

After spending time in the photo albums, I got out my journal that I had kept since before Nathan was born. I was amazed at how much I had forgotten about our lives over those last seven years or so. Once again, this time through my written words, I began to relive the past. I relived the uncertain days leading up to his miraculous birth—what a day of rejoicing that was! Against all odds, we gave birth to a beautiful and amazingly healthy little boy all things considered. A little boy who should be celebrating his seventh birthday who instead is dead after only six and half short years. It just didn't seem possible.

Next in my bizarre birthday celebration, I pulled out Nathan's memory box filled with all sorts of keepsakes I had gathered over the years. Remembrances from birth all the way through his year in kindergarten, many of which I had forgotten about. Some of the things made me smile, others made me cry. And oh, the tears! But somehow these tears were different. They weren't the desperate, agonizing, tormenting kind of tears that I had been shedding lately. These tears were a softer, broken hearted, sad, longing-for-my-son kind of tears. This was my first attempt at "planned" or "intentional" grieving over the death of my son. I actually enjoyed the day and for the first time I didn't feel guilty for doing it. Although I was not answering the phone, a number of family and friends called to leave messages of love and support and many sent cards. Somehow I survived yet another big hurdle in the journey through grief. I couldn't help but feel a little proud and a lot thankful for this small victory.

I've shared how I celebrated Nathan's seventh birthday but I'd be remiss if I neglected to share how Nathan's best friend Stephen, who was only a few months older than him, chose to honor his best buddy's birthday. Any birthday celebration needs a cake and with his mom's help, Stephen created a most unique one. It had LOTS of red icing swished around for the fire hoses and blue icing for the water coming out of those hoses with a big fat number seven candle in the middle. It was perhaps the most beautiful cake Nathan ever had! We shared it together as a family after dinner with Ashley lighting the candle and then blowing it out in honor of her little brother. Stephen also made a cupcake for Ashley as well as one to take to Nathan which Stephen delivered with his mom, Denise, and his sister, Katie. The birthday party came complete with decorations that Stephen "borrowed" from surrounding graves and which his mom insisted he put back. And of course Stephen insisted they

21 The First Birthday

sing "Happy Birthday" to Nathan, the version that was to the tune of Ol' MacDonald that included "cha-cha-cha's" and hiney twisting. When Denise shared the details of Nathan's birthday party I could just see the three of them singing and dancing at his grave! I doubt there has ever been a more bizarre yet love-filled birthday celebration! God had certainly blessed our family with some wonderful but strange friends!

My journal entry on December 7:

Today is Monday, December 7, 1998. Today marks the six month anniversary of my son's death. I don't feel that this is necessarily a milestone one brags about. Although there were certainly days and times I didn't feel I could possibly go on, here I am. Somehow I have managed to survive these past six months without my precious little boy under my feet, in my hair driving me crazy but all the while adding a zest to my life that I find myself longing for again. Yes, it's an anniversary but certainly not an anniversary one celebrates.

Nathan Still a Gift of God

Our First Christmas

My journal entry on December 14:

My heart and mind are full but my ability to get them on paper is questionable. Work is so wild and crazy! Lots of meetings, deadlines, reports, problems etc. things difficult under any circumstances but when you throw a grieving mother into the picture you've got trouble! I feel as if I'm on that edge again and the slightest thing will send me head first into that dreaded pit I struggle so desperately to stay out of. Add to this the holiday season and you've got yourself a fine mess! I feel as if I'm sinking again. Drowning, unable to keep my head above the water. Not really caring or having the energy to fight any more. The holiday season is a tough time anyway and facing Christmas without Nathant seems almost an impossible task this year.

We finally put up the tree. I would typically have it up around Thanksgiving so we would have plenty of time to enjoy it. If it weren't for Ashley, we would have skipped as much of Christmas as possible and we certainly would not have put up a tree. It turned out to not be as traumatic and gut-wrenching as I had anticipated. Instead it was almost too painful for tears. It was without a doubt the most calm tree decorating we had had since Nathan was born. Without Nathan, there was no one to fall into the tree, no one to take the ornaments off as soon as we put them on, no one to get tangled up in the lights or in the garland, no one to fall into the ornament boxes and no one to drop or spill the ornaments all over the floor. It was just the three of us hanging the many ornaments in silence. Few matched. Many were homemade. A number made by the kids themselves. Ashley and Nathan each had their own set of ornaments. Each had a set of the first through fifth Christmas bear ornaments. Each had quite a few from grandparents, family or friends. Dave and I would also get each of them an ornament or two each year symbolic of an interest or milestone. For instance, Ashley had lots of horse and cat ornaments. Nathan had just begun to develop interests of his own but his collection included a number of firemen including a fireman Santa. Our tree would never have won any awards but we would take top prize for being one of the most sentimental trees with a story behind almost every ornament. And as we hung each of those ornaments, it felt as if someone was chipping away at the remaining pieces of my heart. The heaviness of the moment was incredible. The realization that Nathan would not be with us for Christmas hit me like a ton of bricks and it would not let up. It almost didn't seem real. My mind could not quite grasp the concept of Nathan not being there for Christmas, not any Christmas ever again.

    Nathan loved Christmas. You would see the gleam of excitement in his eyes as he would take in all the decorations and activities of the season and especially as he eyed the presents. Oh, how he loved presents! Dave and I seldom bought anything for each other for Christmas. Our greatest gift was watching the children on Christmas morning as we presented them with their hearts' desire (within reason of course). The look on their little faces was priceless! They would even get excited as they watched each other open up their own presents. Again, more wonderful memories! Memories were all we had left of Nathan and Christmas. I wished there were words to describe how sad that reality made me feel. So incredibly sad. And my strategy for Christmas was to simply survive and somehow in the process see that Ashley had the best Christmas she possibly could under the circumstances. Denise let me borrow a cap with the words "Bah! Humbug!!" stamped across the front. That cap described my Christmas spirit to a tee—Bah! Humbug!!

    Christmas is no easy task to tackle under normal

22 Our First Christmas

circumstances. Combine the holidays with a mother's grief and a person is doomed! There were parties at school and church, baking, last minute shopping, family functions in addition to all our normal activities. Add to that the fact that Dave and I were constantly at odds with each other. We finally realized our agitation was not so much with each other as it was our grief rearing its ugly head and we made a conscious effort to cut each other some slack. Once again I found myself struggling mentally and having difficulty concentrating. Even with lists I would have trouble remembering things and staying on task. I could typically function well under stress but that would not to be the case this Christmas. I found myself repeatedly shutting down and not functioning at all. One good thing, being so busy kept me from being consumed by the fact that Nathan was not there to add to the craziness of the season. Life was so crazy for me I decided to take the craziness with me to grief group by wearing my Bah! Humbug!! cap, a sweatshirt that has a crazy looking cat on it that said "Stressed out!", and my footed pajamas. We even brought pictures and shared our favorite Christmas memories at one of our meetings. I don't know how I would have survived the holiday season without my support group! To this day I am so very thankful for that wonderful group of people and what we had together as we tried to make our way through our grief.

On the last day of school before Christmas break, I pulled out of the school parking lot and the tears began to flow. With school out, so much of the busyness was now behind me and so were the distractions that were keeping my grief at bay. I had Dave's present in the car. It was a piece of artwork Nathan had made in his kindergarten class. He had drawn a figure and had his teacher label it "dad" and then he had drawn a recognizable "heart" beside it. Nathan then dictated to his teacher the story behind the picture which she wrote underneath the picture: My Daddy is my friend. It was framed with little cut-out diamond shapes, making it obvious they had been practicing patterning with the colors. I had Nathan's artwork matted and framed for Dave for Christmas. The tears were still flowing when I got to our driveway so I slipped up Peggy's drive instead wanting to show her Dave's present. She just cried along with me.

Ready or not Christmas finally arrived. Christmas Eve was a particularly difficult day for me. Ashley was back and forth between our house and Grandma Peggy's. Peggy invited me down but I refused. I did not feel like being with anyone. So she came to me and we cried and laughed and cried some more. Despite the bad weather, we still went to my family's house for dinner. It was a rather subdued evening. It felt like a strange cloud was hanging overhead, one that everyone knew and felt was there but one that no one wanted to speak about. No one mentioned Nathan although his absence seemed to scream from every direction. We got through dinner and opened gifts leaving as soon as we could. We had done our "duty" more for Ashley than anything else. She seemed to enjoy herself and it was important to keep with tradition as much as possible for her sake. At times, I was almost envious of her and her child like approach to dealing with death.

The next morning there were no yells and screams as there had been the previous Christmas from the little boy in the next room demanding to be unhooked from his dialysis machine so he could get down to the business of opening presents. Or the noises of other Christmases that usually began with a loud thud as he hit the floor followed by the sound of his clumsy run to our room and the inevitable crash as he hit the side of our bed. No begging us to wake up and get out of bed. This year there was only silence. No yells. No screams. No crash. No sweet little voice urging us to get up. An incredibly loud reminder that this Christmas was different. Painfully different. We would never again wake to the sounds that were Nathan. Not on Christmas morning or any other morning.

22 Our First Christmas

Instead, we woke up to the quiet but quick pace of Ashley as she walked across the floor upstairs and down the stairs into our room. Quietly she urged us to get up which we did, for her. None of us knew quite what to do or say. It was so odd without Nathan. So quiet, so calm. So painful. No one dared to speak for fear of releasing that pain into our Christmas morning. We fumbled around nervously. We actually remembered to light our candle in memory of Nathan that I had brought home from grief group for just that purpose. Ashley was eager to get into the packages. Oh, to be a child on Christmas morning! Even in light of the tragedy and pain, there was still that sparkle in Ashley's eyes! But in our eyes were only tears. Poor Ashley didn't know what to do or say to her pitiful parents. We wanted to be excited for her and enjoy Christmas with her but it was more than we could do. We managed to go through the motions as if on automataic pilot and that's the best we could do even for our daughter who we love with all our hearts. I somehow managed to take a few pictures though I dreaded to have them developed and find a set of Christmas pictures without Nathan's smiling face.

Once Ashley was finished with her presents, it was time for Dave to get his. Ashley was excited to have been part of having it framed knowing to some extent how much it would mean to her father. Needless to say he was more than pleased and we proceeded to cry some more. What a Christmas celebration!

Christmas evening we went for the Sours' family dinner. The air was strained, no one knowing what to do or say again. We got through dinner. Then Peggy announced that before we opened presents, we were going to remember Nathan. Well that was all that was needed to break the ice and the tears flowed. Though most of us were not comfortable sharing their memories of Nathan out loud under such conditions, it was still a good thing. Rusty and Tammy gave us a wind chime. A friend had given Tammy one and told her every time she heard it, to think of Nathan being in Heaven and to know he is fine and having a grand time and remember he loves them. So they gave us one with the same instructions. To this day, I never hear a wind chime without thinking of Nathan and the fact he is safe and sound with Jesus. They also gave us a small pine tree to plant in the yard and to decorate in memory of him. A side note: after all these years, the tree still lives. It has suffered ice storms and fungus, lost branches and just like Nathan, grows to its own tune: crooked! By landscaping standards, it should have been removed long ago but we just cannot seem to bring ourselves to take it down. Peggy gave me a "Dollar General" birdhouse to remember all the shopping trips to the dollar store with Nathan. She also bought us a fireman Santa. God is good!

In the wee hours of the following morning, I got up to go to the bathroom. The clock said 2:30 a.m. YES!!! Christmas was officially over! We had survived!!! A great sense of relief came over me! When I got up, I took down the tree and the few decorations I had put up and packed it all away. What a good feeling that was! It was perhaps the first "good" feeling I had had in weeks. That feeling didn't last for long because it was soon replaced with an overwhelming sadness. The kind of sadness you can feel to the bone. I felt like I had backtracked in my grief. I was assured by my support group I was "normal" but what did they know? They were all in the same boat I was! And what is "normal" anyway? I may never know!

I also journaled on December 31:

> *Today is the last of 1998. I feel strangely hesitant to leave 1998 behind. Nineteen ninety-eight is the year Nathan died. It is also the year I last saw my little boy alive.....the year I last held him in my arms......the year I last told him "I love you!......the year he last challenged my authority....the year he last made me laugh at his wild and crazy antics.....the year I last looked upon*

22 Our First Christmas

that mischievous grin....the year is filled with so many "lasts." Nineteen ninety eight will always be the year that changed my life forever. Oh, I've had other "life changing moments" but none to equal the death of my little boy! And I pray that there will not be future "moments" to challenge this one! I also find myself a little eager to be done with 1998. To move on. Move on past the tremendous pain and disappointment and loss it brought to our lives with hopes that the New Year will be different. But then it will be another year without Nathan and the simple changing of the year will not change that in the least.

Nathan Still a Gift of God

Call to Ministry

After the holidays I felt extremely low. I had spent an incredible amount of energy simply surviving them. In addition to feeling wiped out, I was also feeling distanced from God. To be completely honest, my relationship with God had been very strained and distant since Nathan's death. I felt a desperate need for Him but somehow could not seem to get to Him. My heart just was not in it. I would read my Bible and pray but I felt like I was not getting anywhere. There were days and brief periods of time when I would have an overwhelming sense of His presence or of His working in my life but those times seemed few and far between.

In one of our grief support group meetings, we spent a considerable part of the meeting going head to head privately with God. Well, at least that is what my time with Him felt like. As hard as it was, it was a turning point in my relationship with Him. I was still having to really work at my quiet time with Him but I was beginning to feel my time with Him was becoming more personal again rather than just routine.

I began to see that part of my problem with my relationship with God was that I was beginning to have serious doubts about the things I had been hearing from God. God would never use me. I could never write a book or speak or have a full-fledged ministry. I was not equipped to do any of those things. I did not have the education or the time or the know-how to even begin any of these tasks much less bring even one of them to completion. Besides, I was still grieving and tired with little energy or mental ability. Satan was really working overtime on me!

Sunday, January 17, during the evening service, Pastor Dan preached a sermon entitled "When Can't Can." He explained that God had a purpose and a plan for our lives before He even formed us in the womb. He has appointed work for everyone, even me. When God called Jeremiah, his response was "I can't because I'm a child." Just like Jeremiah, I had a hundred excuses about why I could never do the things I felt like God was leading me to do. Dan reminded me that God never calls us to do anything He won't equip us to do. After all, what would be the point of God calling us to do something we could do ourselves? How would He get any glory out of that? All I need to do is say "Yes!" and God will do the rest.

And that evening, that's just what I did. I went forward and asked forgiveness for making excuses. Then with Pastor Dan as my witness, I committed myself and my life to God for whatever job, service or ministry He had for me. I said "Yes!" to God. And I also committed myself to a more intense effort in my quiet time alone with God so He could begin to reveal His plans for me and my life and my future. I also committed myself to strive to be obedient as He revealed those plans. Back in November, I was excited about God "growing me into a new tree." In January, I realized that He could not do that until I said "Yes!" and step out in faith instead of hesitating in fear and uncertainty.

After saying "yes" to God and the call He had on my life for a grief ministry, on January 30, during my quiet time, God gave me the name. "Rescue Ministries" or "Rescue 511." Let me explain. I wanted a name that would honor God and be a tribute to Nathan. Nathan had a love and a fascination with fire trucks and it may sound silly but I started looking up scriptures that had the reference of 911 to see if I could find a scripture for the ministry. No luck. The idea of "Rescue 511" kept popping into my mind. At first, I thought it was silly but it just kept coming and so I started looking up scriptures with the reference of 511 until I came to Job 5:11, "and those who mourn are lifted to safety." I could not believe it! God had given me the name for the grief ministry: Rescue Ministries: Where those who mourn are lifted to safety!!! I cried of course, so overwhelmed by it all! I prayed and thanked God for even considering someone like me for any type of ministry.

I went to work and waited until I thought Dave would be up and coherent enough for me to tell him about my time with the Lord that morning because I wanted him to be the first to know. He was excited although not as excited as me. I felt more than a little embarrassed and silly as I began to share with others what I felt God was leading me to do. But most were not at all surprised especially Pastor Dan who even proceeded to give me some pointers and advice on how to handle a position in the ministry. Two things especially stuck with me. First, I needed to be careful to be obedient and faithful to God and not go off and do things in my own strength because it would meet with certain destruction. Second, I needed to be careful to maintain a fear and awe of God which was exactly where I was, in total fear and awe of what God was wanting to do through me. I could not believe it. The hard part would be in waiting patiently for Him to unfold the plan because this was completely beyond my ability. But my prayer for Nathan's life and death to be honoring to God was coming true beyond my wildest dreams!

24 The Challenges Continue

The Challenges Continue

On January 25, we were out of school due to a threat of icing although it never materialized. Nevertheless, I was grateful to have a day off because I had been wanting to pack away Nathan's things in his room. I had originally thought we would do it as a family and as we went through his things, we would decide what to keep, what to throw away and what to give to someone else who needed it or who would appreciate having something of Nathan's to remember him. We never seemed to be able to get around to it so I decided I would at least pack it all up and then we would go through it later as a family. I really did not think it would be that big of a deal. Actually, I had predetermined in my mind it would NOT be a big deal.

I started with his clothes, forcing myself to approach the task mechanically because I knew if I dared to allow myself to feel anything, I would be a basket case. I also knew I had to act quickly and not take time to think and feel as I packed away all of Nathan's belongings. It was a good plan or so I thought. But it did not take long before I realized how stupid I had been to think I could accomplish such a task without feeling and thinking and remembering.

As I was quickly packing his clothes into a Rubbermaid trunk, my heart was racing and my breathing was rapid and shallow. My chest was tight. I packed even faster. But it was no use. Soon the tears began to flow, slowly and quietly at first. I packed even faster only to find the emotions coming equally as fast. My crying was that frenzied, angry, frustrated kind of sobbing. It took every ounce of strength to continue. But I was on a mission and nothing was going to stop me, certainly not my emotions and tears. I was determined to pack up Nathan's room. My energy was quickly zapped and the crying ended leaving me with such a completely empty and hollow feeling that cannot be described with words. The emotional packing frenzy slowed and I continued with the task at hand. The overwhelming emotions were replaced with a slide show of memories. As I picked up the various pieces of clothing, an image would pop into my mind of a little boy wearing those outfits. They were usually twisted or untucked or on backwards and almost always rumpled in some way, but boy was he cute! I especially struggled as I packed away the Superman, Batman, and Power Ranger outfits. He absolutely loved to dress up in his super hero outfits and did so every chance he got!

As I packed away his toys, an image would surface of a birthday or Christmas present that was ripped open with eager anticipation or there would be a reminder of yet another shopping trip where I had been conned into buying the neatest and latest boy toy! Image after image. Memory after memory of a time that would be no more. Nathan was gone and all that was left was a whole closet full of "stuff." "Stuff" that once belonged to a little boy who enjoyed his "stuff" as much as any little boy could. I know that in the scope of life, "stuff" is not important and one day we will open that closet and decide what to do with all that "stuff" but for the time being it was enough to have it packed away. I was not quite ready to part with any of Nathan's "stuff" and wondered if I would ever be.

As if packing Nathan's belongings were not enough, I get a call that we are getting a new little boy in our preschool. He was a four-year-old named, what else but "Nathan!" I could not believe it! I mean what are the odds?! I really did not expect it to be that big of a deal and I did not give it much serious thought. I went to school with the same attitude I had while packing Nathan's room: "I can do this! I'm tough! No problem!" I actually did fine until around lunch time when once again my energy ran out. I just could not fight it any longer. My Nathan had been in that class for three years and now seeing and hearing the name "Nathan" and knowing it's not his was just more than I could stand. I just had to wonder once again, "Why, God?!" Of all the names

24 The Challenges Continue

in the world, why did God have to bring a little boy named "Nathan" into our classroom?!

I struggled with this and came to realize that I had allowed myself to get back into the familiar routine of not dealing with my emotions and thoughts again. The holidays had taken a big toll on my reserves, as if I had any, and I put up those guards and walls to survive. I was almost too tired and had no desire or energy to face my pain. God, on the other hand, knew that I needed to face my grief head on and a little boy named Nathan was a sure fire way to break down my defenses!

I also realized during one of my many waking moments during the wee hours of the morning that I had allowed myself to believe that I was well on my way to "recovery." Initially, I had so many questions relating to Nathan's death like "Why?" and "What are you doing, God?" God was beginning to reveal a least some of those answers with His call into a grief ministry. I thought that if I had discovered some purpose, some plan for Nathan's death, that somehow facing his loss would be easier if not almost over. WRONG!!! All this time, I had wanted to know "Why?" Now, I realized that knowing at least some of the "why's" does not make the pain any less or the hurt go away. My son was still dead and I still wanted him back and my grieving was by no means over!

February brought lots of doubts and confusion and even fear with the idea of being called to a ministry. I was not sure whether the enemy was messing with me or if I had misunderstood God and His message to me. Certainly, He would have chosen someone more capable. I felt I must have some sort of pride issue to possibly think He would choose me. How could I possibly think I could speak or counsel people or write a book? And I was concerned about what people would think when they found out what I was doing, especially if I were to quit my job for a ministry that did not even exist yet? But that was what I felt God was leading me to do. But how would we make it financially?

Amidst the flood of doubts and second guessing God, He gently reminded me in a Sunday School lesson that the disciples got up and left their nets, their families, their homes, their security to follow Someone they did not really know. God convicted me that I needed to do the same and be obedient to what He was calling me to do despite my long lists of concerns. I needed to lay down my "nets" and follow Him. It was only after this new resolve that Pastor Dan asked me if I were interested in a part-time position at the church working with Nifty and the Family Ministry. There would be a lot of red tape but he asked if I would think about it, talk to Dave, and together pray about the possibility. It was too good to be true! I had only made the decision to be obedient and had not yet followed through and God was already making a way!

On February 21, I went before the Church Council and presented a proposal to take the grief ministry into the community. Up to this point it had strictly been for those within our church. I was a bit nervous but it went well and everyone was very supportive as I shared my call into the grief ministry. The Council passed the proposal unanimously.

Somehow I got the feeling God was going to blow me away with what He's going to do in ministering to the grieving and what a blessing it would be for me to be part of it!

We had a Discipleship Weekend at church in late February. God used the weekend to remind me of the importance of my time alone with Him being in His Word and in prayer especially as I entered into ministry. If I'm to do anything for or with God, I will have to be continually learning and growing in my relationship with Him so it will be Him working in and through me, no me doing things in my own strength. With God in full control of my life, all my worries and "I can'ts" would melt away and the grief ministry would succeed beyond my wildest dreams. I was also reminded that I could do all things through Him knowing He would

24 The Challenges Continue

provide whatever I needed in order to accomplish His will and His call. I simply needed to be obedient and stay in His Word and in prayer.

Through this weekend I also came to a new understanding of God's sacrifice of His Son for me. When I was first pregnant with Nathan, I began to relate in some small human way about what it must have been like for God to give up His only Son to die on the cross. I began to understand the Father's pain to some extent. Through the weekend, I saw Jesus death in a different light. Rather than my understanding of how God felt to lose His Son, I took it one step further and saw that God knows how I feel as I grieve the death of my son. To some, that may bring a response of "Duh!" but to me it was a unique idea I had never considered before. God's Son died and Who better to minister to me than Someone who has been there and understands how I feel?! I took great comfort in that thought. It was definitely a weekend full of reminders and reassurances that I had lost sight of in the midst of my grieving.

But even so, the grief continued. After Mom died, I dreamed about her all the time. In my dreams, she was never dead but always out of the room or away and I was the only one who knew the truth while everyone else in the family went on with their lives believing that she was dead. By the time Dad realized she was still alive it was too late, he had already remarried. Then there were the horrible dreams of how hurt she was when she returned from wherever she had been only to find her "Honey" (Mom's pet name for Dad) had married someone else. But Mom was gracious and continued to live nearby to Dad and his new wife waiting for the day when he would return to her but he never did. I would wake up from these dreams with the oddest feeling that would stay with me for most of the day.

With Nathan, I did not have many dreams at all. I had actually prayed that God would not let me dream about him. When I did have dreams, he was always dead. There was one dream that was especially difficult. I dreamed that I was with Nathan and had just been told he was dead. It seemed like we were at home. He laid so still and had that look I remember so well the day he died, that look of not being there. In the dream I was beside myself with emotion. Then his color improved. He took a breath. There was a small movement. Then more breaths. Very, very slowly he began to come around to consciousness. I could not believe it! Nathan was alive after all! There had been a terrible mistake. But I had to be sure, so I waited. But there was more and more evidence all the time. He was alive. He was weak and groggy from the experience but he was alive! I touched him, I held him. Cautiously at first. I could not believe it! It was as if I had to convince myself that he actually was alive after all. I was almost afraid to believe it. But there he was moving and breathing. The dream was so very real, so real I could feel his skin. I touched him and he was warm. I held him in my arms. I just had to call Charlottesville and tell them the good news! Oh, it was so real. Then, I woke up! I woke up and reality came crashing down on me and my wonderful dream. A dream. That's all it was, a dream. I cried, actually I sobbed. For hours after waking up, I felt a heaviness I cannot describe. It was so real.

Change is Inevitable

On March 6, Andrea and I presented at a Families are Special Too Conference. Our workshop was entitled, "Parent, Child and Teacher Make 3." Andrea and I shared how the three-way relationship impacted the development of a special-needs child in the classroom. I was really nervous and was beginning to wonder if I would be able to do it. In my quiet time on the morning of the conference, God gave me Phillippians 4:13: *I can do all things through Him that strengthens me.* And God did just that! He enabled me to remain calm and share from my personal experiences of what it was like being the parent of a special-needs child and the benefit of working with the teacher and staff as a team. I left feeling pretty good about the session and with a confidence that God would indeed equip me to do what He called me to do.

I finally got up the nerve to inform Andrea I would not be returning to the classroom next year. As hard as it was to hear, she really already knew. I turned in my letter of intent stating I would not be returning as an aide the following year but I would be interested if a position were to open in the field of Assistive Technology. Assistive Technology, or AT, was an emerging field where special-needs children were assessed and then equipped with the various forms of available technology in order to help them overcome their handicapping conditions. That's when the struggle began. I was trying to convince myself and God that I could do both, grief ministry AND an AT position. When the ministry was up and running THEN I could quit my job and focus solely on a grief ministry. Andrea and I were scheduled to meet with Patricia, Supervisor of Special Education in the county, to discuss the details of the AT openings for the next year. I was miserable all week.

On the morning of the meeting, God brought me to the book of Haggai in my quiet time. The book begins with stating how God's people had gotten off track and I was convicted that I had veered away from where I knew God was calling me because of my own desires. It then talks about the people working but having little to show for it. They had neglected the work on the Lord's house and as a result the fruit of their labor was withheld from them. It was time for them to get busy with the work God had given them with the promise that the present house would be greater than the former. And when the people laid the foundation of the temple, He did not wait for it to be finished but began blessing them right away. The book ends with "He has chosen you." I knew what I needed to do, I just needed the courage to do it.

    We met with Patricia and I found myself saying "no" to an offer of a full-time position in AT and working with the Head Start program. Not an easy task turning down a job I would have jumped at the chance to do a year or so earlier! Then Andrea asked if I could work part time and I heard Patricia say "okay." As much as I wanted to say "yes" I knew I had to say "no." I explained to Patricia I felt God leading me into a different direction and needed flexible hours to focus on the ministry to which God was calling me. To my utter amazement, she asked how I felt working independently for the county as a contractor of sorts with flexibility in my hours. When the people laid the foundation, God blessed them! I had laid the foundation to focus on the grief ministry in obedience to God and He immediately blessed me with a job I would equally love and a job that would provide the additional money we needed for our family finances. God is good!

    In the meantime, I needed to focus on finishing the current school year. The annual PTA program proved to be yet another challenge for me. The thought had crossed my mind that this year would be different and the program would go on without Nathan but that was as far as I would let myself go. On the day of the program it became apparent

25 Change is Inevitable

it may just be more difficult than I was anticipating. Here's my journal entry:

> After school, I went home and as I was fixing dinner and getting ready to head back to school, I found my mind going back to last year. We were scurrying around getting dressed, trying to find shoes, tucking in Nathan's shirt for the thousandth time...typical scenario trying to get anywhere for us. This year we had little trouble or chaos getting ready at all. All was fairly calm and rather dull. I shared with Dave my concerns for getting through the evening. He, as usual, said he was sure I'd be fine and gave me a hug. I got in the car and headed down the road. There was no holding back the tears as I remembered what it was like in the car anytime with Nathan...loud and never a dull moment no matter where you were going! Last year the concert was all about colors. And one particular song kept playing in my head because it was the one Nathan would sing in the car the most as they had been practicing it at school for weeks prior to the program. This time, no Nathan...no tune...just silence. Except for the quiet chatter from Ashley and her friend that had come home from school with her. I'm sure they thought I'd stepped over the edge. I didn't care nor could I stop the tears that were flowing down my cheeks.
>
> Last year when we got to school, the kids were to line up in our building with their class. I was in our classroom lining up our kids thinking Dave had Nathan. Only to have Dave come into the room asking where Nathan was. We began a frantic search only to find Nathan exactly where he was supposed to be... lined up with his classmates! Imagine that!
>
> The kids began arriving and we began to line them up. It took every ounce of energy and effort for me not to just run away. And the tears just wouldn't stop. We went into the cafeteria and got the kids on stage. We put our chairs just in front of the stage in case one

of them got a little too close to the edge or needed a friendly reminder that they were to be on their best behavior...two problems we always had with Nathan. We were ever so fearful he would tumble off given his poor balance, and his behavior was always an issue whenever he would realize he had a captive audience! Not an issue this year. The kids did a great job. I sat and tears flowed down my cheeks the entire program. There was no stopping them despite the fact I was in front of an entire audience of people, most of whom would have no earthly idea what the deal was. The kids kept looking at me with puzzled expressions on their faces. They sang songs like "When I Grow Up" and about growing "big and tall" things my little Nathan would never get to experience. Life is just so unfair! The program couldn't be over fast enough for me. As soon as the parents claimed their children, I was out of there! I did it! I survived yet another excruciatingly painful reminder of Nathan's absence. Unfortunately, I knew there would be many more to come.

Some change is not only inevitable but necessary if we are to survive. In mid-March, Dave and I went on another marriage retreat sponsored by our church despite the fact that I had ended up in the ER at the last retreat we attended. We had a wonderful weekend. We had struggled quite a bit in our marriage since Nathan's death. I had been naïve and prideful enough to think after all we had been through while Nathan was alive, we were completely immune from becoming part of the eighty percent divorce rate among couples who have lost a child. It was only a few short months after his death, that I begin to realize it could indeed happen to us as well. Dave and I were grieving very differently as men and women do but also because of our individual personalities. We found ourselves heading in two very different directions and rarely would were able to come together to talk, share, laugh, cry, or remember together. Shortly before the retreat, things had been slowly showing signs of improvement. The retreat brought a lot of things together for us and marked a new beginning in our relationship. We were able to openly share about so many things. It was amazing to see what simply being away from the usual routine and being "forced" to take a good long look at ourselves and our relationship could do. I could actually believe that we were going to make it, not because of anything to do with us, but solely by God's grace.

In addition to what the retreat meant and brought to our marriage relationship, I personally came to a new realization that I later shared with Dave through a letter. I learned I had a tendency to withdraw and isolate myself especially when I am struggling with something. God reminded me that not only was He my refuge but that my husband and my marriage relationship were to be as well. We closed out the weekend by finding and giving a symbol of what the weekend meant to each of us and our spouse, I found and gave Dave a bird's nest to symbolize that God and my husband were my refuge in the midst of the storm.

Nathan Still a Gift of God

Our First Easter

The entire week before Easter, I felt strangely foul. I could not put my finger on it until we were actually into the weekend. Then I realized what my problem was: it was yet another holiday without Nathan. A holiday with more fun and festivities without our little boy there to enjoy them. Easter held so many reminders of losing a son and of death, not that Nathan's death could ever compare to Jesus dying on a cross but nevertheless the reminders were everywhere. The previous Easter, I had taken Ashley and Nathan to buy their Easter outfits. Ashley, of course had to try on her dress to make sure it fit and if she was trying on her outfit, Nathan was certainly going to try on his! He had picked out an olive green pair of pants with a white shirt and matching vest and of course a tie. Oh, how he loved his ties and to dress up! He looked so sharp! It never lasted long because he was such an active little boy. In no time, his shirt tail would be hanging out and his tie would be crooked matching that crooked little grin of his.

None of that this year. Ashley had to have a new dress but we just got her a "new" dress and didn't even call it an "Easter" dress. It was just easier that way. She was also still of the age to want to dye eggs, which we did quickly and quietly on Saturday evening. Ashley was more like her father—neat and meticulous while Nathan really got into dying eggs—literally! None of that excitement this year. On Easter morning Dave and I both felt as if we had the weight of the world on our shoulders. Last year Nathan had gotten a fire extinguisher and a Florida Gators basketball shorts outfit. He loved anything to dress up in and his fascination with the movie *Space Jam* meant a basketball outfit was just the thing. I felt guilty for not making it more special for Ashley this year but I could not bring myself to do anymore than just the basics.

We managed to get ready for church somehow choking

back our emotions as best as we could. My emotions, however, got the best of me in the car on the way to church. Looking out the window, I could not help but notice the beginning signs of spring as we drove into town. But rather than see the beauty, all I could think of was how dare spring come with all the pretty little flowers and how could everything begin turning green and showing signs of life when my little boy was dead. How dare nature and life go on without him! I like the dead looking trees and black mountains. They matched my heart on the inside—no visible signs of life, just dark and grey and depressing.

We had the usual Easter Cantata complete with wonderful songs about life and joy and blah, blah, blah. I really could not tell much about was was said or sung. I was not really there. Besides I did not want to sing happy little songs anyway. Sunday school was even worse. They had planned a little drama presentation and had asked my husband to participate—now get this—as Joseph, Jesus' father! On Easter morning! Dave had fretted a lot over whether to participate or not but finally agreed not wanting to let anyone down. He asked me to help him write something so he could just read it. I told him to just think of how he felt as a father losing his son and to speak from his heart and he would be fine. And that's just what Dave did and it was absolutely wonderful! He got up and spoke from his heart without having any of it written down. Everyone was in tears! And I could not have been any prouder! Dave really has a lot of good stuff to share but it's getting it out that's the problem.

After church, we went to Rus and Tammy's for the annual Sours' egg hunt and cookout. I felt like the day would never end! It was so hard to try and have a "good" time when all I really wanted to do was crawl in a hole and die! But for Ashley's sake, I sucked it up and hid eggs with the kids. The task of meeting her needs helped mask the pain I was feeling inside and before I knew it, it was time to be off to the next event of the day, the Coffey Easter dinner. The fun just would not stop! We managed to eat, be civil, and leave as soon as we possibly could. Thank goodness Easter was finally over! Yet somehow I felt strangely guilty and sad that my grief and pain had overshadowed the wonderful gift God had given me (us) so many years ago but that was honestly how I felt.

I had little time to dwell on my selfish attitude during the Easter holiday because I had to prepare for the upcoming ladies retreat. This proved to be no simple task because of where I was personally. But, by the grace of God, we pulled it off and He proved Himself to be faithful once again. It was a wonderful experience for all those in attendance. I had assumed that because this was basically a repeat from the fall there would not really be anything for me personally through the course of the weekend. Once again I was wrong. During our quiet time with God, I found myself sitting out on the hillside looking out over the mountains. I observed the same beginning signs of spring that were already making an appearance in the valley below making their way up the mountain. I could see tiny little buds on only a few of the trees. Strange but this time I did not feel the same anger I had on Easter morning at the realization that life was continuing despite Nathan's death and my inward pain. This time I saw the hope of new life after the harsh winter and felt God showing me that this was where I was—just beginning to bud, though very sparsely, following the terrible devastation of my "winter" which followed Nathan's death. Hope.

But even with hope, grief had a way of catching me off guard and at times had no rhyme or reason. Our Sunday school class took on the task of having a baby shower for the local Pregnancy Help Center. I was in charge of the games, as usual. Seeing baby stuff truly did not affect me the same way that little boy stuff did and the shower proved not to be a big ordeal for me. But as I left to go home, something hit me. I'm not sure what it was that triggered it but I began to cry, then sob, and before I knew it I was an emotional wreck.

By the grace of God I made it home and managed to pull it together to go inside and face Dave. As I sat with him in front of the TV, we chatted a bit and he made some comment, I don't even remember what it was but I absolutely snapped! I did not ever remember such a strong reaction before. Rage flew into me in a way that I had never before experienced. Dave was of course surprised and had no idea what to do or say, so he did his usual—removed himself from the room. I, however, proceeded to follow him from room to room wanting comfort, understanding, to be held, none of which I got. In retrospect, I believe he was not quite sure what to do or say, if anything. And when he did, it was all wrong. He tried to explain away and dismiss the things I was feeling or thinking as insignificant and unimportant, which only made the situation worse. He finally went into the bedroom to fold laundry even though it was 10 p.m.! It was the only thing he could think of to do under the circumstances to pacify me. I finally gave up and went to bed, which is where he kept encouraging me to go thinking all I needed was a good night's sleep. I did go but I lay there for the longest time sobbing hysterically yet trying to do so quietly so no one could hear. The next day I journaled:

> *It's very hard to put into words how I felt. I was absolutely filled with rage and emotion like I had never before experienced. I felt so out of control. The flood of emotion truly scared me especially the fact that I felt anything but in control. What if it happened again? What if I snapped like that and never came back? I was fearful of "going off the deep end" and ending up in a little padded room somewhere twiddling my thumbs! I know that sounds dumb and irrational but as I said, I had never done this before. I had never felt such rage and emotion. I had never been that out of control before. I felt so uneasy. I found myself carefully guarding how I grieved. I found myself turning off tears...avoiding emotional outbursts and*

26 Our First Easter

> *things that might trigger them...I carefully changed the subject if things got too deep...etc. I was not going to lose it again like that. I quickly fell back into the old routine of stuffing. That's how great my fear is of snapping completely.*

I talked with Dave and told him I was not being critical but if anything like that were to happen again, I needed him to stop what he was doing and simply hold me and let me cry or talk and get it out. I asked him to please not tell me how I should and should not feel or what I should and should not think and do not tell me to go to bed. He agreed. We had definitely come a long way in this journey through our grief.

Nifty came up with the idea for the grief group to have a panel discussion at church to inform people what you could expect from grief by sharing what we had learned from our personal journeys through grief. We all agreed. It turned out to be a wonderful evening. Many in attendance were surprised at how open and honest we were. I think we even surprised ourselves at how comfortable we were sharing our stories and experiences in an effort to educate people about the grief process. I was very proud of our group and of our church for embracing such a ministry.

Nathan Still a Gift of God

In Memory Of

As a memorial to Nathan, a flower garden was planted outside his kindergarten room. It had a number of different shrubs and flowers but one in particular that was notable: blackeyed susans. And of course you know there's another Nathan story coming! Well, Nathan's kindergarten class was walking to the cafeteria for lunch, which meant they walked by our class as we were playing outside on the tricycles and other riding toys. Nathan decided to join us without asking permission. His teacher caught him and tried to get him back on track. Nathan was a very determined little boy and threw a royal fit. Mrs. Elliott sat him down on the sidewalk to try and reason with him. Nathan responded by taking a swing at her and hitting her in the face! You know where this is going! Mrs. Elliott's first name was—you guessed it! SUSAN! Hence, the blackeyed susans in the flower garden! (Even though he didn't literally black her eye.) And by the way, Nathan ended up in the principal's office, where Mr. Chase did his best at giving Nathan a stern talking to about the seriousness of what he had done. Something must have gotten through because that was the last time he took a slug at his teacher! Much to his mother's relief!

We had a good bit of money left over in the Nickels for Nathan account. Dave and I decided to use the money to buy playground equipment for the school. We looked through a number of books that had all sorts of equipment in them, most of which were far too expensive. Then I came across the fire truck—a piece of playground equipment that looked like a fire truck! How wonderful! How appropriate! Of course, we would have to add a little bit to the funds but it would be the perfect thing for us to give back to the school in honor of Nathan and to say thank you for all their support through the years and especially in his death. We got the school's approval and with the help of school staff and a few friends the fire truck was erected and was quite the hit with the kids at school! Our preschoolers were the first to "break in" the equipment. They had been watching the construction for over a week and were filled with questions first about the equipment and then came questions about Nathan. Kids are so precious in their innocence. They asked questions about where he was, did he die, what was he doing. I had to let Andrea handle most of the questions. It was just too much.

The fire truck was dedicated on June 3, the one year anniversary of the day Nathan was admitted to the hospital for transplant. I wrote the following to share with the students and staff, and through tears and emotion I was actually able to read it although Mr. Chase was on standby in case I could not finish:

> Several years ago, we learned our son Nathan was going to need a kidney transplant. We had known since he was a baby that transplant was a very real possibility for Nathan. As we began preparing for the surgery, the staff, PTA and students here at Ladd decided they wanted to do something to help our family with the cost of the transplant and the drugs that Nathan would require following the surgery. So you began a campaign known as "Nickels for Nathan." The children brought in their nickels, dimes and pennies—some even gave up snacks or did chores around the house in order to have money to put in the collection cans in their classrooms. From there, the campaign quickly spread into the community and when all was said and done, over $40,000 had been collected! We were completely overwhelmed by the love and support of our Ladd family and community.
>
> Exactly one year ago tomorrow, Nathan had the long awaited transplant with his father donating the needed kidney. The surgery itself went beautifully but Nathan began having complications as a result of the medications he was receiving. Despite all the doctors' efforts, Nathan died on Sunday, June 7. I can't begin

to tell you how absolutely devastated we were... but again we found ourselves surrounded with love, encouragement, and support from our Ladd family.

And with the money that you collected, we were not only able to cover the expenses of the transplant but also pay off all of Nathan's medical bills from previous years and still have some left over. We began to wonder what we could do with the money that was left in the "Nickels for Nathan" account. After ruling out a trip for two to the Bahamas, we decided to return the money to those who made it all possible in the first place—the children of Ladd Elementary. We quickly decided on playground equipment. As we were going through the catalogs, we found the perfect memorial to Nathan—a fire truck! It was something the kids would enjoy and most of you know how much Nathan loved fire trucks! And it is with much love and gratitude that we give back to you what you have so graciously given to us.

You were there with us as we prepared for Nathan's transplant, you were there for us when Nathan died and our world fell apart, and you're still here for us today as we continue to struggle with our incredible pain and loss.

Most of you know I will not be returning to the classroom next year. I feel God calling me to a grief ministry, which we've already begun at our church. We're calling it "Rescue Ministries: Where those who mourn are lifted to safety." It is my hope that God might use me to help those who are hurting by offering them the same love, support, and encouragement all of you have given to me and my family.

And now we present to you this fire truck. We hope that when you see it, it will bring a smile to your face as you remember Nathan—a little boy with charm beyond his years, a crooked smile, and a gleam in his eye who made it a point to enjoy each day of his life to the fullest!

Nathan Still a Gift of God

And when I had finished reading, Mr. Chase took the inaugural slide.

One Year Anniversary

On June 5, in the midst of the anniversary of Nathan's transplant and death, I journaled:

> Well, here I am right smack dab in the middle of the one-year anniversary of Nathan's transplant and death. Where to start...I've spent most of the last month dreading this week of anniversaries. I really wasn't quite sure what to expect but I just knew it would be tough. I know lots of people have been praying for me (as well as Dave and Ashley) because otherwise I don't think I could've made it this far. I've done far better that I had anticipated. But of course up until today, I've been very busy with end of the year stuff so it's been easy to avoid dealing with my own stuff.
>
> The anniversary was getting closer and closer and brought more and more memories and emotions out. Emotions and memories that I had been able to keep in check. I was becoming more and more tired and unable to maintain the control I was used to. I found myself slipping back into that dreaded pit. I had trouble remembering things and following through with a task. I was tired to the bone all the time. I didn't like going back there again but I had no choice in the matter. It bothered me that a date on a calendar could have such an effect on me, but it did. And no matter how hard I tried to be in control and how much I wanted to do more than just exist, it just didn't happen. The fast approaching anniversary date was in control no matter how much I fought it. I found that my mind flooded with memories of those last few days with Nathan. I was especially haunted with the memories of him at the hospital both before and after surgery.
>
> I can see him so clearly and almost hear him begging not to do the mask...and hear and see his forced breathing and that awful cough while on the

respirator...and those blessed few hours we had with him when he came off that thing...then that horrible night when he began to struggle to breathe and weakly asked for water...haunting memories that right now crowd out all the wonderful memories we have of Nathan's life with us. My heart aches for the way his life ended. Yes, I know it could've been much worse and much more painful. I know he was heavily medicated and didn't suffer. But those days and hours haunt me and probably always will. Fortunately, they hadn't been surfacing until recently. I believe they could drive me mad! As the weekend progresses I suspect they will only get worse. Then my hope is that they'll subside again or I know I'll be a crazy woman!

Saying goodbye to a classroom that held so many memories...to a job that was challenging yet one I had enjoyed...to people I had been with for five years. It was also the week of the fire truck dedication. How would I ever get through this week? I just didn't think it was possible.

But again I know people were praying for me because each day ended to my surprise and relief not having been as bad as I had anticipated. We had our classroom graduation on Wednesday. My mind kept going back two years ago when Nathan was parading around in his graduation cap, dropping it of course numerous times. As usual, he thoroughly enjoyed being in the spotlight. What a happy day that was! Our little boy graduating and going on to kindergarten, a feat we weren't sure would ever happen. Add to that the end of the preschool classroom at Ladd and you have yourself a real tear jerker!

Then came Friday...the last day of school. My last day of work. By this time I was really moving and thinking slow—sometimes not at all! But we managed to pack up most of what was left and say our goodbyes with what tears we had left. We're all sad about what has come to an end. Yet we are excited and anxious,

> *not to mention very nervous at what lies ahead too. I hope and pray that the friendships, especially with Andrea, will continue. We have developed something very special and it would be a shame if we let that slip away. I personally am anxious and excited at the challenges that are ahead for me. I have this wonderful part-time AT position as well as my grief ministry that I want to see grow and flourish. It has also been approved by the Church Council for me to work five to ten hours a week with Nifty. I can't believe all this is happening. Sometimes I feel a little undeserving and a little guilty that all these blessings are coming my (our) way. I find myself waiting for the bottom to fall out. Wondering what catastrophe is waiting for us next. I know that's really pessimistic but that's honest. I'm really trying to take one day at a time and allow God to direct and guide me with all that He's put on my plate. I don't want to get in over my head. And I especially don't want to leave Dave and Ashley completely out of the picture. It's my hope and desire that my family would have more of me and my time. I've neglected so much in the past few years and in particular the last year or so. Yes, some of it is understandable, but I need to work on my priorities and get them straight once and for all with God being the first and foremost.*

My journaling continued as the anniversary approached:

> *Today is Sunday, June 6, 1999. It is a little after 4 p.m. This time last year, Nathan was just being taken off the respirator. Now one year later, I sit here and still feel the pain and the hurt of that day. That terrible day when our son died. So much has happened in the last year, the year since his death. It's hard to believe it's been a whole year since he died. Sometimes it seems like another lifetime ago. That life with Nathan is a thing of the distant past. Other times it seems like only yesterday. The pain is still there although*

> different now...not quite so stinging and sharp... except for recent days. The hole that his death left in our life will never be filled. Sure we've managed to go on living, but life is so different now. He brought so much excitement and joy and laughter and challenges to our lives...we'll never be able to replace any of that. We have seen some of the purposes for his death and some positive things happen as a direct result of his death, but even with all that, it still sometimes doesn't make any sense and nothing will ever take away the pain of the tremendous loss.
>
> I know I must go on...God has things for me to do...things that I never would've been able to do had it not been for the life of a little boy named Nathan. And yes, things that I would've never been able to do had it not been for his death. It is hard sometimes to understand and accept God's plan. I really struggle... really struggle...with this one on a regular basis. Some of it I will never understand until I get to Heaven. That's probably the biggest comfort I have most days. That one day I will get to Heaven and see my precious little boy!

After revisiting that day of one year ago, I felt an overwhelming urge to go to the cemetery. I had not been back since the day of the funeral. Some said that was okay while some thought it odd and still others felt like I was avoiding and having trouble with closure. I felt like it was the latter myself. Visiting the cemetery somehow made it final. I admit I was more than a little nervous and uncertain what a trip to the cemetery might bring but I thought it better to find out by myself than wait until the following day when I would go with Dave and Ashley. I was especially concerned about how my reaction might affect Ashley who was already uncomfortable with my moods and emotions.

I decided to take a more scenic route along the Blue Ridge Parkway. The sun was absolutely gorgeous streaming down through the trees and the occasional views of the

28 One Year Anniversary

valley below and the distant mountains were beautiful. I was amazed that I could see the beauty all around although a part of me still did not want to acknowledge it was there especially as I made my way to my son's grave. It somehow did not seem right that everything was so beautiful. I arrived at the cemetery, parked the car, grabbed some tissues and headed for Nathan's grave. When I arrived, I found a once beautiful but now faded Christmas wreath, a large cardboard sign painted with the words "we love u" printed on it and nailed into the ground, an interesting little cross made of an assortment of pieces of wood that had been nailed together and painted with green and tan. It, too, was nailed to the ground. There were also a few pieces of silk flowers, obviously retrieved from the woods or maybe surrounding graves. It was obvious that Nathan's friend Stephen had been there! I looked around and decided to have a seat leaning up against the headstone that was at the foot of Nathan's grave. The grass on his grave was still rather sparse so I could tell exactly where it was. The sun was still shining brightly only this time shining down on me. There were birds chirping and flying around. Even a butterfly. I could hear the occasional car passing by. The little church that I grew up in sat upon the hill overlooking the cemetery. Strange. There I was sitting at my son's grave and not crying. I did not even feel the urge to cry. Instead, I felt such an incredible peace. I tried to get a sense of Nathan somehow. I knew we had buried him there. But Nathan was not there. Oh, I know his body was there but I knew for certain that Nathan was not there. I felt a sense of yet another chapter of life—my life and Nathan's life—closing. It was time for me to move on. I knew there would still be days of incredible pain and hurt and tears from missing Nathan but I also knew that despite the pain, or maybe because of the pain, I had work I needed to be about. Work that would make Nathan's life and death somehow seem worthwhile. I felt God's presence and reassurance that He was there—had been there and would continue to be there. Odd how the very thing and place I had avoided for almost a year could bring me such peace and comfort, but it did.

The following day was June 7, the one year anniversary of Nathan's death. Dave, Ashley and I had decided to spend the day together. It started off rather awkward with none of us quite sure what to say or do. It was 10:30 a.m. before we had any kind of a plan. (That was our first mistake, not having a plan in place BEFORE the day arrived.) We decided to go to the cemetery first thing and get that over with so we did not have that hanging over our heads all day. Then came the decision as to what to do after that. Ashley was the only one brave enough to make a suggestion and being only nine years old, she suggested going to Sherando Lake. I really did not want to go to the lake but I did not have a better idea so after further discussion, disagreement, and a display of ugly attitudes, we were off.

We had placed flowers in church on Sunday and we took those to place on Nathan's grave. Ashley had made a cardboard sign while at the Thomas' which said "we miss you Nathan." We arrived at the cemetery and were uncomfortable as we got out of the van and made our way to the grave. We surveyed together the items I had found there the day before. We set the flowers at the foot of the grave and Ashley nailed her sign into the ground. I did not feel the same peace and comfort as I had felt when I was there the day before, largely because of how much it hurt to see Dave and Ashley so upset. But I still did not have a sense of Nathan's presence there. We did not stay long. There did not seem to be a reason to stay. We decided to take the parkway home, the same route I had used the day before. It was another beautiful day and we rode in silence which I was determined to break. I asked Ashley what she missed the most about Nathan. She, being so much like her father, did not have an answer. So, I said I missed his giggle and his "hi-yah!" (Nathan loved to make karate moves and sounds!)

28 One Year Anniversary

Dave said he missed his smile. We talked some about what a stinker and a joy he was. I asked Dave if he remembered much about those days in the hospital and in particular the day Nathan died. He was a bit groggy about those first days but he remembered all too well the day he died. I asked if he thought he could ever put into words how he felt that day and what thoughts went through his head but I did not get a definitive response though I would still love to know how he perceived that day as a father and as a man.

We also discussed plans for a headstone. Dave suggested a fire truck with a superman "S" on it. Ashley suggested a superman carrying a fire truck. We really needed to stop talking about it and do it. Dave had told me a couple weeks prior that I was putting off the headstone because it made it final and that I was avoiding closure—yes, my Dave said that! I knew he was right.

We drove into town to get Ashley a snorkel for the lake. We stopped by the house and ate lunch there, ditching the idea of a picnic at the lake. That was just too much. While at the lake, Ashley seemed to enjoy herself. Dave obviously was not much into it. I did not even get in the water past my knees, instead sitting in the shade and watching and listening to the people. My heart was too heavy to have fun. We finally went home.

I had specifically requested that we spend the day together as a family. However, when we got home, Dave proceeded with his plans to work on the garage he had started building, which I think was as much therapy for his own grief as anything. And not only did he work on the garage, but he invited a number of people over to help. I slipped away to my upstairs hideout and stayed there until I was sure everyone was gone. I was not even answering the numerous phone calls from friends and family checking on us and letting us know they were thinking of us. In hindsight, I can see that we should have made more solid plans for the actual anniversary day. Dave is not the type to fly by the seat of his pants and not having a definitive plan made him nervous and so he resorted to his own method of dealing with things, which was work. I, on the other hand, was "comfortable" spending the entire evening on the couch upstairs wallowing in a very deep pit of depression. I was getting a bit concerned about myself and wondering how far and how long before I need to do something about the mental and emotional state I was in much of the time. But at least we had the first year behind us at that point and that was quite an accomplishment. I was unsure of what the next year would hold but I would just continue to take it one day at a time.

Following the day of the anniversary, I journaled the following:

> *Today is Tuesday, June 8, 1999. Well I did it! I survived the one year anniversary of Nathan's death! Quite a feat in my book! I will admit that the week of anniversaries relating to transplant and his death wasn't as horrid as I had anticipated. And I know it was a direct result of the prayers of so many people that got me through.*

More New Beginnings

July 1, 1999, Dave started his own computer business after quitting his job of thirteen years with another company. We had talked the idea to death and I felt it was God's will but Dave was not quite sure. After dinner out to discuss the whole thing again, we had driven separately and on the way home I prayed that God would show Dave His will for him in starting his own business. By the time I got home, Dave was just finishing up with a phone call that resulted in him finally realizing that him starting his own business was indeed God's will for him and the time was now. He turned in his notice and with only $1,000 in our savings account, he ventured out on his own without a single customer or job scheduled because Dave believed he needed to build his own clientele rather than take from his previous job. I was certain people thought the grief had finally taken its toll on us and we had obviously lost our minds with both of us quitting our steady-income jobs. It was scary to say the least, but we knew we were both following God in obedience and trusted God to provide. And boy, did He ever! Almost immediately Dave became a different person, more relaxed and more easy going as he was living his dream of being his own person.

On July 8, I had quite a surprising realization. For the first time since Nathan had died, I felt a real sense of peace and joy in living. I actually realized as I was driving to work that the sun was still shining! Everything was especially bright and beautiful as the sun was shining after the rain we had the night before. With work, I felt like I was becoming a functioning human being again. I felt like I was not only able to do my job but to find a joy in doing it again. It was a really good place to be. A place I never thought I would be again. It did not last long but I felt it. If I felt it once, then the odds of feeling it again were good. Slowly but surely I was coming to believe that life would somehow be full again.

Not ever in the same way and maybe not to the degree it was before. Life had a huge hole in it without Nathan fitting into the scheme of things. But I was beginning to believe his life and even his death were driving me and molding me into something new and different and maybe even something exciting. I was seeing signs and evidence of it almost every day. Life was so very different now. Sometimes it seemed like life with Nathan and all he brought to it was another lifetime ago. Sometimes it was almost hard to remember the chaos we existed in with him, but it was a chaos I would have given anything to be back in the middle of! It is funny how we never really appreciate what we have until it is gone. But that life can never be mine again so I have no choice but to look forward to whatever it is that lies ahead.

My journal entry on July 17:

> *After surviving the anniversary of Nathan's death, I have since come up out of that dreaded pit but am left with a keen sense of Nathan's absence. Last summer I was in that shock & numb phase and much about his death and its reality didn't register. This summer as we go to the lake or have a cookout his absence seems to scream at me. The intense emotions are gone but that sense of emptiness and longing for his presence have taken their place. I don't know which I prefer really. I wonder when one really comes to terms following the death of their child or if they ever really work it out in their head and in their heart. At this point, I think the only thing to do is to somehow come to terms with the pain and loss and accept the fact that they will always be there to some degree or another. I don't believe that there will ever come a day when I don't have to acknowledge their presence. That would mean I would not acknowledge Nathan's absence—and I don't ever think there will be a day that his absence is not a very real and painful reality.*

My journal entry on August 29 at the start of the new

29 More New Beginnings

school year:

> The new school year started without Nathan again. Ashley went off into the fifth grade—boy is that hard to believe! On the way to school, there were moms and dads all along the road sending off their kids—especially kindergartners. I traveled back in my mind to that first day of school when I took Ashley to kindergarten and Nathan to preschool and then left them both there with almost complete strangers! It was one of the hardest things I had to do up to that point in time. It seemed like only yesterday. Now Nathan had been dead for over a year and Ashley went off to fifth grade and didn't even need me to walk her in! Life is so different now. I will say that this year was easier than last year for me. I guess those people who say the "first time" of doing things without your loved one is always the hardest. I hate it when "they" are right! It still makes me sad when I think about Nathan and life going on without him. I wonder what he would look like. If he would have gotten much taller. I wonder if he would be reading. I wonder what mischief he would be up to. I wonder if he would still be giving me a run for my money—yeah! Somehow I think he would've always done that until I was old and gray! Gosh I miss him so much! His smile! That gleam in his eye! His giggle! Some days it seems so hard to comprehend that he's truly gone... never to come back. Other days it's getting harder to remember exactly what life was like with him here. It seems the more time passes, the farther and farther I leave him behind. That makes me sad. I don't want to leave him behind! I want him here...NOW! I've told several people that I almost feel like I have two people living inside me. One is sad and lonely and misses her little boy so much and the way life used to be. The other is thrilled with the direction her life is taking and the things she is doing and so excited to see how God is working. I wonder if one day these two people

> will merge into one or if I'll always experience these two incredibly different sets of feelings.

The fall was filled with numerous conferences and events. Perhaps the biggest was my trip to Nashville for the American Association of Christian Counselors Conference held at the Opryland Hotel. The conference is for professional and lay counselors as well as pastors who minister to those who are hurting. It provides education and training on how to be better people helpers but it also provides wonderful speakers and times of worship to replenish the hearts and minds of those who are always giving to others. I came away from the conference with so much but will share just a few of the more profound messages and moments from the conference. Dan Allender, a Christian counselor, author, and speaker, talked about how we all have a story and how we have to be with our story and to take ownership of it. He also talked about having themes in our lives that mold us, make us, and take us where God wants us to be. Evil works to destroy us and our faith, hope, and love but God uses those same circumstances to grow us in our faith, hope and love. He said the absence of faith is the refusal to remember the past and God in it. Hope looks to the future we have as a result of our faith and the past. I was to ask myself: Why has my past happened? How will the meaning of my story play out for me, for others, and for God?

Then Joni Eareckson Tada spoke with such openness and honesty about her struggle with God and how she thanked God for her wheelchair and for how it had kept her dependent on Him and close to Him. She wouldn't want to give it up if it meant she would lose closeness with Him.

And finally the most profound moment in the whole conference came during an evening of praise and worship. Charles Billingsley was singing "I Bowed on My Knees and Cried Holy." This song had special meaning because my family was singing it together around the time of my mom's

29 More New Beginnings

death. Of course, he probably didn't get ten words out before I was sobbing! I thought it was just another "link" moment to go back and remember the pain and acknowledge that it's still there—but no-o-o-o!!! I felt God asking me to praise Him. What?! You have got to be kidding me! I must have misunderstood. But God was indeed saying to me, "Praise me! I want you to praise me in Nathan's death." No way! I've gotten to a point I could pray—truly pray and read the Bible and have a strong vital relationship with Him. I could even praise Him for what He was doing in my life and could recognize the positive results of Nathan's death. I could see his death and my grief and pain had brought me to an incredible place in my life but PRAISE GOD FOR NATHAN'S DEATH??! No way! Not gonna do it! God replied, "I didn't say 'for,' I said 'in.' I want you to praise me in Nathan's death." I still could not fathom praising God for or in! I couldn't! I wouldn't! But that was exactly what He was asking. I do not know how long the battle raged but eventually God won out. I still don't know how but somehow I summoned every ounce of strength in my being to raise my hands in praise of God in Nathan's death. Somehow with that first tiny movement, the strength to completely raise my hands just came. And so there I was lifting my hands and praising God in Nathan's death! What an incredible step that was for me in my relationship with God and in my healing!! Of course, I had to do even that in His strength, not my own, but I did it! I did it! And more than that I meant it! I was truly able to praise God in that moment for Nathan's life and in his death.

After the conference in Nashville, the following weekend was Camp Dragonfly which was the first annual grief camp for kids hosted by the local hospice. I volunteered as a counselor and Ashley went as a camper. I had to be there on Friday for training and orientation with the kids coming on Saturday and going home on Sunday. I had the "bumblebees" or kindergarten through second grade little girls. It was a great weekend and a wonderful experience for the fifty or so kids that came. The only thing it lacked in my opinion was a focus on God.

I then went to a Women of Faith conference where I enjoyed a good time of singing and praising God, which I had not done in quite some time. I guess the pump had been primed in Nashville!

Then I had my first meeting with the grief committee at U.Va. that I had agreed to serve on with several other parents and grandparents who had children who died. It was difficult going back to the seventh floor but not as difficult as I had anticipated. I even did a quick stroll by the playroom and the PICU and NICU. That proved to be a bit much, too many memories. Our meeting went well and we had the beginning plans for a one-day workshop to help other parents with the loss and grief following the death of a child.

Then we had our Fall Revival with speaker Rev. Tim Hight. I missed Sunday but went on Monday. I was feeling pretty proud of my recent accomplishments and felt certain that I would not be required to work further on myself or my relationship with God! So I looked around and began wishing and praying for those around me and what THEY might get out of the evening! Ha! Well, the more he talked the more he got on MY toes! Hey wait a minute! What about all I the work I've done on myself in the past weeks and months?! Well, God saw it differently and despite all the work I had done, there was still more. And so work I did for another three nights! Of special interest was Tuesday night as he was talking about God's grace. He told a story of a man who went to Heaven and was taking a tour. He came to Grace Street and all along the street there were nothing but garages. When he asked why, it was explained that these were God's search and rescue vehicles. Whenever anyone came to know Jesus or was in need of His grace, God would send out a search and rescue vehicle to aid that

29 More New Beginnings

person. And then what does Rev. Hight do? He pulls out a toy rescue vehicle with a working siren and tells us that the next time we hear a siren, we're to think of God's grace, God's search and rescue that is available to us any time and in any situation. What a kick in the pants that was! I shared with him afterward about Nathan's death and how much he loved fire trucks and sirens and whenever I saw or heard one I immediately thought of Nathan. Now when I hear or see one maybe I'll think of Nathan AND God's grace to see us through the most difficult time in our lives and know God continues to send out His search and rescue for us.

My journal entry on November 25:

> *This fall has been an absolutely incredible journey for me! I've already gone in to detail elsewhere so I won't repeat myself. Perhaps one area of the biggest struggle for me right now is doing God's will. Sermons, scriptures, comments from people, Sunday school lessons all seem to be convicting me of the same thing...I'm not in God's will...at least not completely and to the place He wants me to be. I came to a realization that the joy I had experienced resulting from my work was only to be short lived. As much as I believe that God brought me to this place and to each of the things I am doing, He did not intend for them to fill the void in my life. Although I certainly tried to use them that way! The joy that I had experienced (for the first time on July 8) was not a lasting joy. Only God can provide that lasting, deep down, inner joy...not jobs or anything else. And nothing I could do or have or experience in my own power could ever take away the pain and emptiness left by the death of my son.*
>
> *My AT job especially has been absolutely overwhelming for me the past few weeks! With that, my church job, doing the books and paperwork for Dave's business, home, family, church, and my grief ministry, I feel like I can't keep my head above water!*

> *Something has to give! I feel like it needs to be my AT job. Yet I struggle giving up something that I believe God gave me to do. It is a wonderful feeling to help kids, teachers, and parents with a child who has special needs do something or communicate where they couldn't before. And I love my job and the sense of fulfillment it brings. And why would God give me all this experience with special needs kids if I'm not going to have the opportunity to use it?*

Another November journal entry:

> *Well here we are again! Another Thanksgiving without Nathan! I will admit that I don't feel as rotten as I did last year. Last year I spoke of "an ache in my heart that won't go away." That still remains true to this day. As the holidays and Nathan's birthday began approaching I found myself against my will being plagued by an overwhelming void and emptiness. A "funk" as I refer to it has settled down, around, and in me that I can't seem to shake. I can't say that it's an emotional thing but rather a fog...a void...a "funk." No matter what I try to do to make it go away, it's still there. I feel trapped in this "funk" unable to get out. I can say that I have lots to be thankful for this year and I actually "feel" thankful unlike last year's struggle to be sincere about giving thanks. But despite having things and people and events in my life for which I am extremely thankful for, I still don't have the one thing I want more than anything...Nathan. And I'll never have him here with me ever again. It's so hard to adjust myself and my life to that fact. Even harder I think is to adjust myself and my life and be happy about it.*

Time Goes On

My Dad and Lynn gave me a new Bible for Christmas. *The Woman Thou Art Loosed Bible* which includes devotional material written by T. D. Jakes. On January 9, 2000, two devotional statements from that Bible spoke to me: 1) *Now that God has brought you through the crisis and raised you up to maturity, you are ready to enter into the fullness of His destiny for you.*[116] And, 2) *Your eyes have not yet seen; and your ears have not yet heard; and neither has it entered into your heart all the things that God has prepared for you! Now is the time to see, to hear, and to believe. Now is the time for blessing.*[117]

On January 12, God spoke to me through Isaiah 46:3-4:

> [3]*"Listen to Me, O house of Jacob, and all the remnant of the house of Israel, who have been upheld by Me from birth, who have been carried from the womb;* [4]*Even to your old age, I am He, and even to gray hairs I will carry you! I have made and I will bear, Even I will carry and will deliver you"* (NKJ).

There was also a statement from *Woman Thou Art Loosed*: *The images, scars and victories that we live with have shaped us into the people we have become. We will never know who a person is until we understand where they have been.*[118] Another word from the same Bible came on January 13: *God is a restorer. That is to say as you sit by the fire sipping coffee rehearsing your own thoughts playing old reruns from the scenes of your life—some things He will explain and others He will heal.*[119]

On January 26, God gave me Hebrews 5:8, which speaks of Jesus: *though He was a Son, yet He learned obedience by the things which He suffered* (NKJ).

In April, Ashley was baptized after publicly going forward during one night of revival. Her testimony is that she had previously asked Jesus into her heart during a magic show in AWANA, but being a rather shy child, she had never shared that with anyone or made her faith public. During revival, she very nervously went forward and, after being counseled by Miss Maggie and her flannel graph, was baptized.

On the first Saturday of May, the grief committee I was serving on at U.Va. held our first grief workshop for parents who had experienced the death of a child. There were several parents, even a grandparent, that worked on the various aspects of the day. My role was primarily to lead the small group discussion around various topics relating to grief, its effects, the journey through it. We even had a session about where God was in our grief. It was a wonderful day and I was thrilled to have yet another avenue to share with other parents who were grieving about the death of their child and offer them hope.

If you remember, I was sensing I needed to resign from my assistive technology job. I wrestled with the logic of that but finally truly felt that was what God wanted me to do. I resigned by email on Sunday night and was offered a full-time position at the church on Monday! God already had it covered. He was waiting for me to trust him and to follow in obedience.

On June 24, I journaled about the two-year anniversary of Nathan's death:

> *I'm not sure what I was expecting but it certainly wasn't what I got. The closer the anniversary got, the lower I got until I was completely numb. I managed to take care of routine tasks and pretty much operated on automatic pilot most of the week. Needless to say, I got through the week without much event. By weekend, I had begun to come out of my "funk" and the fog began lifting.*

On September 26, I journaled a small comment about "knowing" Nathan was going to die:

30 Time Goes On

> *About two years prior to Nathan's death piece by piece I began seeing that Nathan was going to die. At first, I thought I was crazy...pessimistic...no hope. But the more I sought God, the more I began to realize this was for real even though I held out until the very end that I was wrong and I had misread God's messages to me over those two years. Unfortunately, His messages were all too clear and true.*

The following journal entry comes on December 2, Nathan's birthday:

> *Today, Nathan would be nine years old and would be excited about going to dinner at his restaurant of choice and then on to the parade to see the fire trucks...but he's not...he's dead. My little boy is dead. And life goes on...and on...and on...without him. When does it get easier? Does it ever get any easier? I keep waiting....it never happens. I was talking to Tammy who dropped by today to bring me a plant (which unfortunately I'll probably kill) and to say she remembers and hurts with me. She said that a friend who lost her daughter says that the third is the hardest. As I think about that, this is what I've decided...the first year is hell—you're just trying to survive. The second year stinks but is better than the first so you begin to think "I've got this thing beat!" Then you discover you have to do everything all over again the third year, and the fourth, and the fifth...*
>
> *So here I sit wondering what my little boy would look like now?...what would he be interested in?...how tall would he be?...would he still be a handful?...would I still be pulling my hair out?...My heart is breaking to not have him here with me. And to think his little body is lying in the ground and it's so cold and dark...I can hardly bear the thought. I spent all his life caring for him...making sure he was okay...fighting to keep him alive...to see that life was as normal as it could be...to keep him warm and safe...I have good, happy*

> *thoughts of past birthdays, holidays, school, typical life days, but they're interrupted by thoughts of his little body lying in the hospital, his cold body in the coffin. He lived life "wide open" and those images of him in death are so haunting...so unreal...so painful.*
>
> *Every part of me screams out for him (silently of course). Oh, how I long to hold him, to squeeze him, to kiss on him, to laugh at and with him, to fuss at him and then turn my head so he couldn't see me smile. Why does life have to be this way? Why does it have to hurt so much? Why my son? Why so soon? All questions that I can't seem to find answers to. And even if I did have all the answers, it wouldn't change anything...Nathan would still be dead and I would still forever feel the pain of losing my son.*

On December 18, we were preparing for the funeral of a church member and dear friend, Jack. Jack loved Nathan and would often take him home after church for lunch and a ride on his lawn mower. While a familiar song from Third Day was playing, the funeral director and his crew were arranging the casket and the flowers in preparation for the funeral and "something" hit me like a ton of bricks. I ran and hid in my office and cried and cried. The instant I heard Dave's boots hit the top of the stairs outside my office door, I ran and motioned him in. We were sitting side by side and I just did not feel close enough and so I climbed up on his lap until it was time to go in for the service. We sat in the back and did okay until the slide show of pictures of Jack's life. It was all over then as we watched a number of pictures of Nathan on the lawn mower and others with him and Jack. We were sobbing by the time all was said and done. It was amazing how much it could still hurt.

2001 To Present

On February 16, 2001, I journaled:

> So much is happening (as usual) and I just can't seem to find the time to get all my thoughts down. This week I made a connection with where I'm at and how God is working to heal my heart. My heart was hardened and I was in control of who got in and what got out. No one was ever able to completely get in until I had children. God gave me Ashley and Nathan and, in the process, opened up the pathway into my cold heart for the first time in a very long time... farther than anyone had ever gotten in before. Then, Nathan's ordeal only continued to tear away at the walls and barriers although I remained very much in control of other's getting in and even more in control of how much came out. Then he died. The walls I had worked at all my life were blown to bits. Without my usual protection I withdrew into myself and away from those closest to me. I couldn't let them see the real me nor could I risk letting them into my world with my defenses so weakened. I was very lonely. It was then that God began a major renovation of my heart. He has enabled me and taught me to love people with a compassion and empathy and sympathy and genuineness that I never knew possible. And He's teaching me to acknowledge, label, and express my heart to others in a way that I've never been able to do before. His love is now able to flow through me and into others. It is a miracle! And the work is no where near over! There's much left to be done in giving me the heart He desires me to have in order to be used by Him in the work He's given me to do. And the greatest part of all this heart stuff is that I am discovering for the first time in my life what it means to have an intimate relationship with God. Now I'm just beginning to tap into this new idea and level of relating to Him but I can tell already it's going to be

wonderful!

All this is very choppy and is in no way relating what I mean for it to say. But I had to get the gist of it down before the newness of this revelation wears off. It hit me when we were asking ourselves in widows group "how are you a better person for having known your loved one that died?" I felt I needed to be as vulnerable and open as they were and so I began sharing and this is what came out! I don't know what God has in store for me even this afternoon, but I do know He is working diligently to renovate my heart, soul, mind, and body in order that I might glorify Him and minister to others. The process is "killing" me but the results are incredible!

Late July, on a Friday I had some time alone and knew I needed to spend that time with God. I sat down and in no time I found myself on my knees and on my face asking God to forgive me for my stubborn and rebellious nature, not one hundred percent sure what that confession was all about. I asked Him what it was I needed to do. He immediately made it clear to me that I needed to complete the draft of Nathan's headstone on the computer. It was time I closed the book on that aspect of Nathan's death. It had been far too long and was not only affecting me but Dave and Ashley as well. They needed it and I was delaying it. I completed the task in only a few minutes actually because Dave, Ashley, and I had already decided what to include on the headstone, I just needed to put it together on paper so they could order it. On the front, we of course had his name, date of birth, and date of death. We had a small cameo picture of him placed at the top, the one of him on the tricycle that was taken by the newspaper reporter for an article about the transplant only a week before he died. We also had Isaiah 65:18, *We will rejoice forever in that which God has created* at the bottom, which was the verse from the card we received when he was born. Then, on the back we had them put a fire truck, a Superman "S," Taz, Bugs Bunny, and a Batman symbol. We also had the chorus of "Our God is an Awesome God" by Rich Mullins inscribed on it: "Our God is an awesome God, He reigns from Heaven above, With wisdom, power and love, Our God is an awesome God."

Once I completed the draft, I continued journaling:

> *Then it was back to God. That's when the reality of what I had just done and what it said hit me. The wailing and crying out in pain and agony over the life and death of Nathan came with power and intensity.... it started with stating how I was feeling and had felt over the years...how tired I am...how unfair it was that he suffer like that...all the pain, the surgeries, the procedures, the infections...and then to die. I just wanted to be like Elijah and curl up under a tree and die. I'm that tired and that weary...just let me die. It's just too much. Then the why's came...why did mom have to die? Why the miscarriages? Why the difficult pregnancy? Why did Nathan have to be sick? Why all the pain and agony his entire life? Why did he have to die? Why? It's just too much! I give up! I can't go on! I won't go on! Just let me die! Then I felt like Elijah in the cave—I'll just run and hide in a cave. But God finds him/me even there as I sit in emptiness and darkness and loneliness. Then I give up...I give up...I can't do it any more...I give up. "Help me Father. I can't make it on my own."* (Then, as I'm praying, I visualize in my mind) *And He reaches down and takes me up in His arms—I'm almost completely lifeless with the agony and weight of all the pain. He holds me and comforts me and quiets me. I begin thanking Him and praising Him for who He is and all that He's done in my life and continues to do. Even in and through all the pain and even Nathan's death. Then He sets me on my feet and says it's time to come out of the cave. It's time to come out and be about what He's called me to do.*

Late September, I realized after reading a book on spiritual leadership that God had called me to be a "leader"!!! I knew he had called me to minister to people but I never really thought of it as a call to leadership. It gave the calling a much more intimidating twist. I was so very humbled to think He would call me to such a task.

They, whoever "they" are, say it takes three to five years to reach a "new normal" following the death of a loved one. June 2003 marked the five-year-anniversary of Nathan's death. So had I reached my "new normal" in life? As much as I hated to admit it, I had and "they" were right! I don't know the exact moment it happened. Actually I think it was much more a process, albeit a very painful one, to be where I was at the five-year point.

On June 1, 2003, I journaled:

> I can't help but note the date and consider my life in these last five years. How different life is...how different I am. Five years ago we were getting ready for Nathan's transplant. Today we're getting ready for a graduation of a young lady we didn't even know five years ago (We had taken in a sixteen-year-old whose mother had died.) We're considering a ministry with the youth at church. Ashley's now a ninth grader! Dave has his own business. I'm on staff at church. God is indeed good! God does heal. He restores. He is faithful. He is my strength, my hope, my joy, and my comfort.

On June 10, 2005, I journaled:

> The seven-year-anniversary of Nathan's death has come and gone. I say it every year (all the time) but I just can't believe it's been seven years! Although sometimes life with him seems so incredibly far away. I "celebrated" by speaking to John's doctoral students about grief and its effect on families on June 8. (Our friend John Thomas had become a professor

at Liberty University.) *I thoroughly enjoyed being with the doctoral students—Intimidated at first but after all was said and done, they were very warm and receptive and responsive. A little girl from Love (The little mountain community I grew up in was actually called "Love.") speaking to doctoral students on grief! Only God! I visited Nathan's grave on Tuesday. Ended up prostrate on my face in the grass before the Lord surrendering to Him all that I am and have. And praising Him for what He has done, is doing, and is going to do in my life. He is so incredibly awesome—just like the chorus on the back of Nate's headstone. I also started writing (again!) Nathan's story on Tuesday. Have been feeling It's "time" and thought most appropriate on the day of the seventh anniversary. I feel as if I've entered my promised land. My promised land of ministry. I'm considering school—this time much more clear on path and know the delay has been until I could see more clearly my calling to pastoral counseling/care. My ministry is to be through the church—not be a licensed counselor in a clinic. And the other thing is that I've needed to realize I don't need the degree in order to do what God calls me to do. The degree will only better equip me and open more avenues for me to minister in. We'll wait and see what comes of all that. In the meantime I very much move forward with what God has for me without excuse and without reservation or hesitation. And it's Him I choose to trust and depend on.*

On December 24, 2005, I journaled:

Christmas Eve—I can't help but think of Mom—she would be sixty-one today and of course Nathan would be fourteen, and I can only imagine what he would be like as a teenage boy! I'm as guilty as the next person holding out that this season should somehow bring a reprieve from all that brings sadness and from struggle—a time that should bring peace if only for a

> *brief time. But with that unrealistic expectation only comes a heavier sense of loss and loneliness. Any peace to be had can only come from Jesus Christ and that peace is available all year long—I really don't have to wait for that one time a year to have anything—I can have it all throughout the year.*

December 2, 2006, I journaled:

> *Nathan would be fifteen today. Hard to believe he's been dead for so long! Yet it's been so long it's hard to....not sure how to say what I mean—he's been dead longer than he lived—our lives have been without him longer than we had him—it's weird—and yes, still sad.*

What About Today?

As I write this, it's been twelve years since Nathan died. Even though it's been twelve years and even though I've reached that "new normal" and even though I have found joy in life again, I still grieve the loss and especially the physical absence of my son in my day-to-day life. I think no matter how long I live, I will always grieve Nathan to one extent or another. I certainly know that he is far better off where he is and I know he is safe and waiting for our arrival in Heaven some day, but the human side of me, the mother in me, still grieves. And I think that's ok—it's part of my new normal.

So exactly where are we today? At the writing of this, Dave and I are both forty-five years old, we will soon celebrate twenty-four years of marriage. Dave just celebrated his eleven-year-anniversary being in business for himself selling and servicing computers. He still enjoys fishing, hunting, and golfing. He misses Nathan and having a son by his side in these and other things but God has blessed his life with a number of young boys and men to pour his time and self into over the years. One such avenue coming by way of teaching the middle school boys Sunday school for quite a few years. However, Dave's finally graduated as he and I are currently teaching a young co-ed class.

Ashley is twenty-one years old and a senior at Bryan College, a small Christian college in Dayton, Tennessee. She plays on the volleyball team and is majoring in biology though still doesn't know exactly where God is leading her with that. She married her high school sweetheart, Michael, this past summer. They will live on campus in married housing as they complete their education. Dave and I both welcome Michael into the family, already feeling as if we are gaining a son rather than losing a daughter.

And what about me? It was only several years into the grief of Nathan's death and I was having my quiet time with my morning coffee in hand as I sat in the swing on our front porch. I felt God asking me if I could have Nathan back, would I? But in doing so it would mean I had to give up all I had come to know of Him and who I had come to be in Him. With that in mind, would I have my son back? Without thinking or missing a beat, I felt myself immediately respond, "No, Lord. I wouldn't have Nathan back if it meant I had to give up all I have in You." Then I burst into tears at the horror of what I had just said! What a horrible mother I must be! But horrible or not, I meant it. I certainly wouldn't have "signed up" for my son to die if given the choice on the front end, but where I was as a result of walking this path, I would not go back and undo it either.

I recently celebrated my eleven-year-anniversary being on staff of Wayne Hills Baptist. What started as a grief ministry with one small grief support group has multiplied to a ministry where I provide individual, couple, and small group lay counseling for our church members as well as for people from the surrounding community. I also provide assistance to other local churches to establish their own support groups for grief and other issues. I conduct workshops on grief and other life issues and speak to various groups as God opens up doors of opportunity gladly sharing how God has worked in my (our) life (lives). What started as a "grief ministry" has now grown and evolved over the years to the point I felt a name change was necessary. Shortly after the tenth anniversary of Nathan's death, I registered the new name "Isaiah 61 Ministries" believing God has called me to help people find their healing, wholeness and freedom in Christ from the griefs and traumas in life with the ministry being founded on Isaiah 61:1-4:

> [1]"*The Spirit of the Lord G*OD *is upon Me,*
> *Because the* L*ORD has anointed Me*
> *To preach good tidings to the poor;*
> *He has sent Me to heal the brokenhearted,*

32 What About Today

> To proclaim liberty to the captives,
> And the opening of the prison to those who are bound;
>
> ²To proclaim the acceptable year of the LORD,
> And the day of vengeance of our God;
> To comfort all who mourn;
>
> ³To console those who mourn in Zion,
> To give them beauty for ashes,
> The oil of joy for mourning,
> The garment of praise for the spirit of heaviness;
> That they may be called trees of righteousness,
> The planting of the LORD, that He may be glorified."
>
> ⁴And they shall rebuild the old ruins,
> They shall raise up the former desolations,
> And they shall repair the ruined cities,
> The desolations of many generations.

And as I minister to people, Nathan's story continues to unfold. No matter how long I live, there will always be a place in my heart that still grieves for my baby boy, and even in that, Nathan's story continues. As long as God allows me to continue to minister as a result of all we've been through, our gift of God keeps on giving and Nathan's story keeps unfolding. So how do I end *this* part of his story? How do I bring this book to a close? In the process of working on the very first draft, I felt like God gave me the answer to that question. And so I leave you with the words I wrote at my computer less than forty-eight hours after Nathan's death. I still marvel at how the words just flowed that day. There was no editing. No hesitating. It was as if the words had to come out. I just sat and began to type and didn't stop until the words did. These same words were read a few days later at Nathan's funeral. And these same words bring to a close this chapter of Nathan's story:

Nathan Still a Gift of God

Almost seven years ago, Dave & I were faced with a very difficult decision. We were twenty weeks pregnant when we found out our unborn child had a very serious medical condition. We had three choices: to do nothing and our baby would almost certainly die, to abort, or we could choose an experimental surgery to be performed on our unborn child. After further testing we were told that even with the experimental surgery, our unborn child had only a one in four chance of survival and even then there would probably be significant brain damage as well as deformities. There was also no way to know for sure the extent of damage to the lungs and whether they would be able to support life. We chose to do everything humanly possible to give our child life and leave the results in God's hands. With all the odds against us and our unborn baby, we chose to do the experimental procedure.

Over the next weeks and months, our pregnancy was closely monitored. Then on December 2, 1991, we found ourselves getting ready for an emergency C-section. The delivery room was filled with doctors and nurses waiting for a very sick little baby. There was complete silence as the delivery took place. Then the most beautiful sound filled the room......it was the sound of our newborn son crying at the top of his lungs! God defied medical science and gave us a son we named Nathaniel which means "gift of God." During the next hours and days and weeks, we discovered that our son was NOT brain damaged......he was NOT deformed, and his lungs were fine! Nathan did, however, suffer significant damage to his entire urinary system.

The next few years were rather medically involved with frequent hospital stays, numerous infections, a number of surgeries and medical procedures, lots of blood work and testing and many trips to the doctor. It was a very difficult time in our lives but God provided us with everything we needed every step of the way.

32 What About Today

Nathan became more stable and was finally able to go to school to address his developmental delays which were a result of his extensive medical involvement. At two-and-a-half years old, Nathan attended the Early Childhood class at Ladd Elementary. Nathan blossomed! He went in barely walking and hardly talking. Then before we knew it, he was running around and into everything and was never quiet! Nathan never failed to amaze us with his ability to overcome the odds.

A couple of years ago, Nathan had surgery to reconstruct his bladder which had been damaged in utero. He had a severe reaction to the drugs he received both during and after surgery for sedation and pain management. He almost died. We had faced many trials and obstacles over the years with Nathan's medical condition with some very intense moments but this was the first time we had to face the very real possibility of losing our son. But Nathan once again beat the odds and came out on top! However, Nathan's renal function began to fail. We fought very hard to avoid the inevitable. But it became necessary to begin making plans for transplant. However a few weeks before the scheduled surgery, Nathan came down with a nasty virus and prevented us from going ahead with the surgery. We continued with our efforts to avoid dialysis but last August we had no choice but to begin peritoneal dialysis. Following the surgery to place the catheter for dialysis, we were able to do the dialysis at home and after some adjustment it soon became a routine way of life. We began preparing once again for the day Nathan would receive his transplant. Time passed very quickly and all the pieces began falling into place. We soon had an actual transplant date. As with every big event in Nathan's life, we and many others spent much time in prayer. We knew without a doubt it was God's will for us to proceed with transplant despite an unexplainable feeling that things were going to be different for

Nathan this time. The big day arrived. It was a long day. Family and friends rallied around us in love and support as they've done for us so many times before. After a very long day, we received word the surgery was over, everyone was fine, and Nathan's new kidney was working like a charm!

The next hours and days were busy and filled with challenges but the outlook was promising. On Saturday afternoon, we were overjoyed when Nathan was removed from the respirator and began waking up. Being a typical male, the first thing he requested was the Cartoon Network and the remote! But it wasn't long before he wanted to know where his daddy was and we quickly made the arrangements to bring dad up to visit his son. We had a wonderful few hours together with Nathan. Despite everything, Nathan had once again been able to make the most of his circumstances. Dad returned to his room and everyone was elated over the events of the past few hours.

Some time later, Nathan began having trouble breathing and was soon placed back on the respirator. Instead of improving, things only got worse. There was nothing for me to do but to go downstairs to the chapel and pray. I spent a long time there reading various passages of scripture and talking with God. We have been through many, many difficult situations with Nathan and God always reassured us everything would be alright. God didn't do that this time and I left the chapel knowing that it was only a matter of time before God would take our son home to be with Him.

We spent a long night and day waiting as Nathan's doctors and nurses did everything in their power to save our son. Their efforts failed and Nathan died late Sunday evening.

Nathan had only a few short years here on earth. Even before he was born, God had a plan for Nathan and He has used Nathan to impact people wherever he

32 What About Today

went. He faced trials, obstacles, pain, and discomfort that many people never see in an entire lifetime. Nathan faced his adversity head on. No matter how bad the circumstances, Nathan could always find something to smile and giggle about. For a six-year-old, Nathan had an uncanny way with people and could easily have them wrapped around his little finger in a matter of minutes. As a result, Nathan has more friends than one could count. Nathan has a family who loves him very much. He has a father, mother, and sister who love him more than words could express! We never ceased to be amazed at the things our little boy would do or say!

Seven years ago we had a decision to make. Had we been able to look into the future and see what the next seven years would hold, would we have made the same decision? Absolutely!

Nathan Still a Gift of God

"Nathan"

By Ashley Sours, age 11

When the little baby was born,
No one thought he would live.
But God, He had a plan for him,
And Nathan gave all the joy he could give.

All the while Nathan grew,
We knew God had a plan,
For Nathan faced death a couple of times,
But still he amazed every man.

Every day with him was a joy,
Even though I didn't show,
How it was to be his big sister,
To love and care for him so.

He was never really mad at me,
But he did have his times,
When he managed to get into my room,
To get out I would give him a dime.

When I got the call,
That my little bro' was dying,
All I could think of at that moment was why,
And to try to keep from crying.

The first few days my brother was gone,
All you could be was sad.
But I was assured that he was in Heaven,
And then I could only be glad.

32 What About Today

And one day when I get to Heaven,
I will see him face to face.
And then we will talk for hours,
In that AWESOME place!!

But until I get up there,
To see him in the sky,
I will live by faith down here,
With Jesus by my side.

Jesus is here to comfort us,
As we go along the way.
Until we see our little Nathan,
On that very special day!

Nathan Still a Gift of God

Photos

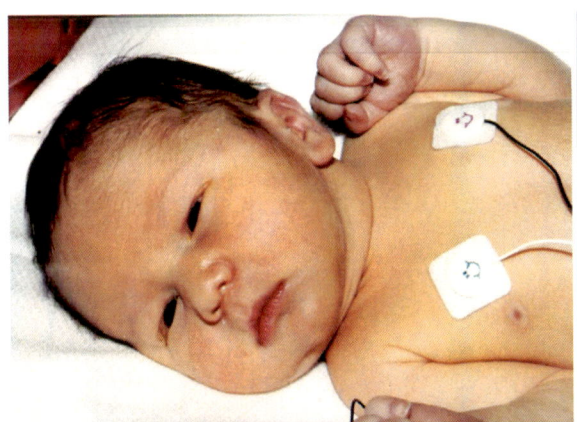

Nathan's first days of life

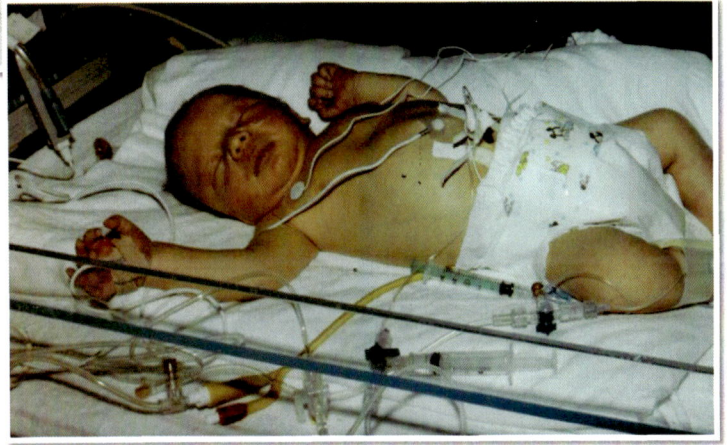

All wired up in the NICU

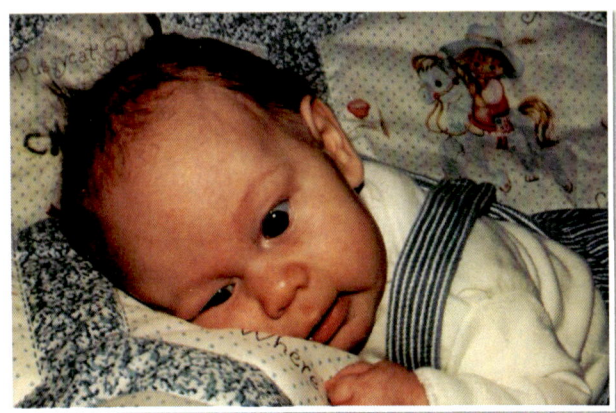

Sweet Baby!

Nathan Still a Gift of God

Even a feeding tube can't spoil Easter with Ernie

Nathan's second Christmas

Family vacation at the beach

Photos

Nathan and Ashley in a Little Tykes car

Nathan turns two

Nathan and Ashley licking the ice cream beater

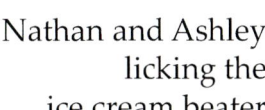

239

Nathan Still a Gift of God

Our little angel and mouse (his shirt reads: "Around here I'm the Big Cheese" — and he was!)

Nathan and his ride

Christmas at Grandma's

Playing at the park—2 days before transplant

A handsome ringbearer for his Uncle Mike's wedding

Nathan's favorite Bible character: "Golilah" (his confusing the stories of David & Goliath and Samson & Delilah)

Nathan and Ashley with their cousins Ben, Sara, Jessica, Bethanne and Keri

We love Granddaddy's motorcycle!

Ashley and Nathan with their new kittens

Appendix
Scripture Section

1) Psalm 30: [1] *I will exalt you, O Lord, for you lifted me out of the depths and did not let my enemies gloat over me.* [2] *O Lord my God, I called to you for help and you healed me.* [3] *O Lord, you brought me up from the grave; you spared me from going down into the pit.* [4] *Sing to the Lord, you saints of his; praise his holy name.* [5] *For his anger lasts only a moment, but his favor lasts a lifetime; weeping may remain for a night, but rejoicing comes in the morning.* [6] *When I felt secure, I said, "I will never be shaken."* [7] *O Lord, when you favored me, you made my mountain stand firm; but when you hid your face, I was dismayed.* [8] *To you, O Lord, I called; to the Lord I cried for mercy:* [9] *"What gain is there in my destruction, in my going down into the pit? Will the dust praise you? Will it proclaim your faithfulness?* [10] *Hear, O Lord, and be merciful to me; O Lord, be my help."* [11] *You turned my wailing into dancing; you removed my sackcloth and clothed me with joy,* [12] *that my heart may sing to you and not be silent. O Lord my God, I will give you thanks forever.*

2) Psalm 31: [1] *In you, O Lord, I have taken refuge; let me never be put to shame; deliver me in your righteousness.* [2] *Turn your ear to me, come quickly to my rescue; be my rock of refuge, a strong fortress to save me.* [3] *Since you are my rock and my fortress, for the sake of your name lead and guide me.* [4] *Free me from the trap that is set for me, for you are my refuge.* [5] *Into your hands I commit my spirit; redeem me, O Lord, the God of truth.* [6] *I hate those who cling to worthless idols; I trust in the Lord.* [7] *I will be glad and rejoice in your love, for you saw my affliction and knew*

the anguish of my soul. ⁸You have not handed me over to the enemy but have set my feet in a spacious place. ⁹Be merciful to me, O Lord, for I am in distress; my eyes grow weak with sorrow, my soul and my body with grief. ¹⁰My life is consumed by anguish and my years by groaning; my strength fails because of my affliction, and my bones grow weak. ¹¹Because of all my enemies, I am the utter contempt of my neighbors; I am a dread to my friends—those who see me on the street flee from me. ¹² I am forgotten by them as though I were dead; I have become like broken pottery. ¹³For I hear the slander of many; there is terror on every side; they conspire against me and plot to take my life. ¹⁴But I trust in you, O Lord; I say, "You are my God." ¹⁵ My times are in your hands; deliver me from my enemies and from those who pursue me. ¹⁶Let your face shine on your servant; save me in your unfailing love. ¹⁷Let me not be put to shame, O Lord, for I have cried out to you; but let the wicked be put to shame and lie silent in the grave. ¹⁸Let their lying lips be silenced, for with pride and contempt they speak arrogantly against the righteous. ¹⁹ How great is your goodness, which you have stored up for those who fear you, which you bestow in the sight of men on those who take refuge in you. ²⁰ In the shelter of your presence you hide them from the intrigues of men; in your dwelling you keep them safe from accusing tongues. ²¹ Praise be to the Lord, for he showed his wonderful love to me when I was in a besieged city. ²² In my alarm I said, "I am cut off from your sight!" Yet you heard my cry for mercy when I called to you for help. ²³ Love the Lord, all his saints! The Lord preserves the faithful, but the proud he pays back in full. ²⁴Be strong and take heart, all you who hope in the Lord.

3) Psalm 138: *[1] I will praise you, O Lord, with all my heart; before the "gods" I will sing your praise. [2] I will bow down toward your holy temple and will praise your name for your love and your faithfulness, for you have exalted above all things your name and your word. [3] When I called, you answered me; you made me bold and stouthearted. [4] May all the kings of the earth praise you, O Lord, when they hear the words of your mouth. [5]May they sing of the ways of the Lord, for the glory of the Lord is great. [6] Though the Lord is on high, he looks upon the lowly, but the proud he knows from afar. [7]Though I walk in the midst of trouble, you preserve my life; you stretch out your hand against the anger of my foes, with your right hand you save me. [8]The Lord will fulfill his purpose for me; your love, O Lord, endures forever—do not abandon the works of your hands.* The footnote: *Beware of taking God's provision and answered prayer for granted. As you make plans and dream dreams talk with God about them. God works out his plans for our lives and will bring us through the difficulties we face.*

4) November 12, Isaiah 6:1-8, 11-13: *[1]In the year that King Uzziah died, I saw the Lord seated on a throne, high and exalted, and the train of his robe filled the temple. [2]Above him were seraphs, each with six wings: With two wings they covered their faces, with two they covered their feet, and with two they were flying. [3]And they were calling to one another: "Holy, holy, holy is the Lord Almighty; the whole earth is full of his glory." [4]At the sound of their voices the doorposts and thresholds shook and the temple as filled with smoke. [5]"Woe to me!" I cried. "I am ruined! For I am a man of unclean lips, and I live among a people of unclean lips, and my eyes have seen the King, the Lord*

Almighty." ⁶Then one of the seraphs flew to me with a live coal in his hand, which he had taken with tongs from the altar. ⁷With it he touched my mouth and said, "See, this has touched your lips; your guilt is taken away and your sin atoned for." ⁸Then I heard the voice of the Lord saying, "Whom shall I send? And who will go for us?" And I said, "Here am I. Send me!" ¹¹Then I said, "For how long, O Lord?" And he answered: "Until the cities lie ruined and without inhabitant, until the houses are left deserted and the fields ruined and ravaged, ¹²until the Lord has sent everyone far away and the land is utterly forsaken. ¹³And though a tenth remains in the land, it will again be laid waste. But as the terebinth and oak leave stumps when they are cut down, so the holy seed will be the stump in the land."

(Endnotes)

Chapter 8 Season of Preparation

1   Henry T. Blackaby and Claude V. King, *Experiencing God: Knowing and Doing the Will of God*, (Nashville, Tennessee: Lifeway Press, 1990), back cover.

2   Matthew 9:28-29 ²⁸When he had gone indoors, the blind men came to him, and he asked them, "Do you believe that I am able to do this?" "Yes, Lord," they replied. ²⁹Then he touched their eyes and said, "According to your faith will it be done to you."

3   Acts 3:16 *By faith in the name of Jesus, this man whom you see and know was made strong. It is Jesus' name and the faith that comes through him that has given this complete healing to him, as you can all see.*

Appendix and Endnotes

4   2 Corinthians 4:8-9 *[8]We are hard pressed on every side, but not crushed; perplexed, but not in despair; [9]persecuted, but not abandoned; struck down, but not destroyed.*

5   Romans 8:26-27 *In the same way, the Spirit helps us in our weakness. We do not know what we ought to pray for, but the Spirit himself intercedes for us with groans that words cannot express. And he who searches our hearts knows the mind of the Spirit, because the Spirit intercedes for the saints in accordance with God's will.*

6   1 Peter 5:10 *And the God of all grace, who called you to his eternal glory in Christ, after you have suffered a little while, will himself restore you and make you strong, firm and steadfast.*

7   Matthew 14:28-33 *[28]"Lord, if it's you," Peter replied, "tell me to come to you on the water." [29]"Come," he said. Then Peter got down out of the boat, walked on the water and came toward Jesus. [30]But when he saw the wind, he was afraid and, beginning to sink, cried out, "Lord, save me!" [31]Immediately Jesus reached out his hand and caught him. "You of little faith," he said, "why did you doubt?" [32]And when they climbed into the boat, the wind died down. [33]Then those who were in the boat worshiped him, saying, "Truly you are the Son of God."*

8   Psalm 27:13-14 *[13]I am still confident of this: I will see the goodness of the Lord in the land of the living. [14]Wait for the Lord; be strong and take heart and wait for the Lord.*

9   Jonah 2:9 *But I, with a song of thanksgiving, will sacrifice to you. What I have vowed I will make good. Salvation comes from the Lord."*

10   Matthew 13:58 *And he did not do many miracles there because of their lack of faith.*

11   Matthew 15:27-28 *[27]"Yes, Lord," she said, "but even the dogs eat the crumbs that fall from their masters' table." [28]Then Jesus answered, "Woman, you have great faith! Your request is granted." And her daughter was healed from that very hour.*

12   Luke 18:43 *Immediately he received his sight and followed Jesus, praising God. When all the people saw it, they also praised God.*

13   Romans 8:32 *He who did not spare his own Son, but gave him up for us all--how will he not also, along with him, graciously give us all things.*

14   Hebrews 10:23, 35-36 *²³Let us hold unswervingly to the hope we profess, for he who promised is faithful. ³⁵So do not throw away your confidence; it will be richly rewarded. ³⁶You need to persevere so that when you have done the will of God, you will receive what he has promised.*

15   Genesis 15:6 *Abram believed the Lord, and he credited it to him as righteousness.*

16   Genesis 21:7 *And she added, "Who would have said to Abraham that Sarah would nurse children? Yet I have borne him a son in his old age."*

17   Genesis 22:1 *Some time later God tested Abraham. He said to him, "Abraham!" "Here I am," he replied.*

18   Genesis 30:22-23 *²²Then God remembered Rachel; he listened to her and opened her womb. ²³She became pregnant and gave birth to a son and said, "God has taken away my disgrace."*

19   Genesis 35:10 *God said to him, "Your name is Jacob, but you will no longer be called Jacob; your name will be Israel." So he named him Israel.*

20   Genesis 43:1 *Now the famine was still severe in the land.*

21   Exodus 2:23-25 *²³During that long period, the king of Egypt died. The Israelites groaned in their slavery and cried out, and their cry for help because of their slavery went up to God. ²⁴God heard their groaning and he remembered his covenant with Abraham, with Isaac and with Jacob. ²⁵So God looked on the Israelites and was concerned about them.*

22   Exodus 6:6 *"Therefore, say to the Israelites: 'I am the Lord, and I will bring you out from under the yoke of the Egyptians. I will free you from being slaves to them, and I will redeem you with an outstretched arm and with*

mighty acts of judgment.

23   Exodus 6:9-12 *⁹Moses reported this to the Israelites, but they did not listen to him because of their discouragement and cruel bondage. ¹⁰Then the Lord said to Moses, ¹¹"Go, tell Pharaoh king of Egypt to let the Israelites go out of his country." ¹²But Moses said to the Lord, "If the Israelites will not listen to me, why would Pharaoh listen to me, since I speak with faltering lips?"*

24   Exodus 13:17-18 *¹⁷When Pharaoh let the people go, God did not lead them on the road through the Philistine country, though that was shorter. For God said, "If they face war, they might change their minds and return to Egypt." ¹⁸So God led the people around by the desert road toward the Red Sea. The Israelites went up out of Egypt armed for battle.*

25   Exodus 14:13-14 *¹³Moses answered the people, "Do not be afraid. Stand firm and you will see the deliverance the Lord will bring you today. The Egyptians you see today you will never see again. ¹⁴The Lord will fight for you; you need only to be still."*

26   2 Corinthians 1:3-4 *³Praise be to the God and Father of our Lord Jesus Christ, the Father of compassion and the God of all comfort, ⁴who comforts us in all our troubles, so that we can comfort those in any trouble with the comfort we ourselves have received from God.*

27   2 Corinthians 4:11 *For we who are alive are always being given over to death for Jesus' sake, so that his life may be revealed in our mortal body.*

28   Isaiah 48:10-11 *¹⁰See, I have refined you, though not as silver; I have tested you in the furnace of affliction. ¹¹For my own sake, for my own sake, I do this. How can I let myself be defamed? I will not yield my glory to another.*

Chapter 9 Life's Never Dull
29   Luke 22:32 (Jesus talking) *"But I have prayed for you, Simon, that your faith may not fail. And when you have turned back, strengthen your brothers."*

30   Deuteronomy 1:2 *(It takes eleven days to go from Horeb to Kadesh Barnea by the Mount Seir road)*

Nathan Still a Gift of God

31   Deuteronomy 1:22-40 (Passage tells story of Moses sending the twelve spies into the Promised Land and because of their fear, brought back a report that the land could not be taken.)

32   Deuteronomy 7:22-23 *The LORD your God will drive out those nations before you, little by little. You will not be allowed to eliminate them all at once, or the wild animals will multiply around you. But the LORD your God will deliver them over to you, throwing them into great confusion until they are destroyed.*

33   Deuteronomy 8:10, 12, 14, 16-18 *^{10}When you have eaten and are satisfied, praise the LORD your God for the good land he has given you. ^{12}Otherwise, when you eat and are satisfied, when you build fine houses and settle down, ^{14}then your heart will become proud and you will forget the LORD your God, who brought you out of Egypt, out of the land of slavery. ^{16}He gave you manna to eat in the desert, something your fathers had never known, to humble and to test you so that in the end it might go well with you. ^{17}You may say to yourself, "My power and the strength of my hands have produced this wealth for me." ^{18}But remember the LORD your God, for it is he who gives you the ability to produce wealth, and so confirms his covenant, which he swore to your forefathers, as it is today.*

34   Deuteronomy 9:23 *And when the LORD sent you out from Kadesh Barnea, he said, "Go up and take possession of the land I have given you." But you rebelled against the command of the LORD your God. You did not trust him or obey him.*

35   Deuteronomy 20:1-4 *^{1}When you go to war against your enemies and see horses and chariots and an army greater than yours, do not be afraid of them, because the LORD your God, who brought you up out of Egypt, will be with you. ^{2}When you are about to go into battle, the priest shall come forward and address the army. ^{3}He shall say: "Hear, O Israel, today you are going into battle against your enemies. Do not be fainthearted or afraid; do not be terrified or give way to panic before them. ^{4}For the LORD your God is the one who goes with you to fight for you against your enemies to give you victory."*

36   Daniel 3:25 *He said, "Look! I see four men walking around in the fire, unbound and unharmed, and the fourth looks like a son of the gods."*

37   1 Thessalonians 3:3 *so that no one would be unsettled by these*

trials. You know quite well that we were destined for them.

38   Joshua 13:7 "and divide it as an inheritance among the nine tribes and half of the tribe of Manasseh."

39   1 Corinthians 2:4-5 *⁴My message and my preaching were not with wise and persuasive words, but with a demonstration of the Spirit's power, ⁵so that your faith might not rest on men's wisdom, but on God's power.*

40   Joshua 21:43-45 *⁴³So the LORD gave Israel all the land he had sworn to give their forefathers, and they took possession of it and settled there. ⁴⁴The LORD gave them rest on every side, just as he had sworn to their forefathers. ⁴⁵Not one of their enemies withstood them; the LORD handed all their enemies over to them. Not one of all the LORD's good promises to the house of Israel failed; everyone was fulfilled.*

41   Judges 3:1 *These are the nations the LORD left to test all those Israelites who had not experienced any of the wars in Canaan.*

42   Judges 7:10-11 *¹⁰"If you are afraid to attack, go down to the camp with your servant Purah ¹¹and listen to what they are saying. Afterward, you will be encouraged to attack the camp." So he and Purah his servant went down to the outposts of the camp.*

Chapter 10 Season of Testing

43   *Life Application Bible*, New International Version, (Wheaton, Illinois: Tyndale House Publisher's, Inc. and Grand Rapids, Michigan: Zondervan Publishing House, 1991), 431.

44   1 Samuel 1:7 *This went on year after year. Whenever Hannah went up to the house of the LORD, her rival provoked her till she wept and would not eat.*

45   1 Samuel 1:10 *In bitterness of soul Hannah wept much and prayed to the LORD.*

46   1 Samuel 2:1-2 *¹Then Hannah prayed and said: "My heart rejoices in the LORD; in the LORD my horn is lifted high. My mouth boasts over my enemies, for I delight in your deliverance. ²"There is no one holy like the LORD; there is no one besides you; there is no Rock like our God.*

47   *Life Application Bible*, New International Version, (Wheaton, Illinois: Tyndale House Publisher's, Inc. and Grand Rapids, Michigan: Zondervan Publishing House, 1991), 447.

48   1 Samuel 9:3 *Now the donkeys belonging to Saul's father Kish were lost, and Kish said to his son Saul, "Take one of the servants with you and go and look for the donkeys."*

49   1 Samuel 13:11-12 *[11]"What have you done?" asked Samuel. Saul replied, "When I saw that the men were scattering, and that you did not come at the set time, and that the Philistines were assembling at Micmash,[12]I thought, 'Now the Philistines will come down against me at Gilgal, and I have not sought the LORD's favor.' So I felt compelled to offer the burnt offering."*

50   1 Samuel 14:8-10   *[8]Jonathan said, "Come, then; we will cross over toward the men and let them see us. [9]If they say to us, 'Wait there until we come to you,' we will stay where we are and not go up to them. [10]But if they say, 'Come up to us,' we will climb up, because that will be our sign that the LORD has given them into our hands."*

51   1 Peter 1:6-7 *[6]In this you greatly rejoice, though now for a little while you may have had to suffer grief in all kinds of trials. [7]These have come so that your faith—of greater worth than gold, which perishes even though refined by fire—may be proved genuine and may result in praise, glory and honor when Jesus Christ is revealed.*

52   Luke 22:44 *And being in anguish, He prayed more earnestly, and His sweat was like drops of blood falling to the ground.*

Chapter 11 Growing Health Concerns
53   *Life Application Bible*, New International Version, (Wheaton, Illinois: Tyndale House Publisher's, Inc. and Grand Rapids, Michigan: Zondervan Publishing House, 1991), 503.

54   2 Samuel 7:5 *"Go and tell my servant David, 'This is what the Lord says: Are you the one to build me a house to dwell in?'"*

55   2 Samuel 10:12 *"Be strong and let us fight bravely for our people and the cities of our God. The Lord will do what is good in his sight."*

56   *Life Application Bible*, New International Version, (Wheaton, Illinois: Tyndale House Publisher's, Inc. and Grand Rapids, Michigan: Zondervan Publishing House, 1991), 583.

57   Ibid., 581.

58   Ibid., 584.

59   Ibid., 585.

60   2 Kings 5 (The story of Naaman)

61   *Life Application Bible*, New International Version, (Wheaton, Illinois: Tyndale House Publisher's, Inc. and Grand Rapids, Michigan: Zondervan Publishing House, 1991), 616.

62   2 Kings 7:1-2 [1]*Elisha said, "Hear the word of the Lord. This is what the Lord says: About this time tomorrow, a seah of flour will sell for a shekel and two seahs of barley for a shekel at the gate of Samaria."* [2]*The officer on whose arm the king was leaning said to the man of God, "Look, even if the Lord should open the floodgates of the heavens, could this happen?" "You will see it with your own eyes," answered Elisha, "but you will not eat any of it!"*

Chapter 12 No Other Option
63   2 Chronicles 7:4-5 [4]*Then the king and all the people offered sacrifices before the Lord.* [5]*And King Solomon offered a sacrifice of twenty-two thousand head of cattle and a hundred and twenty thousand sheep and goats. So the king and all the people dedicated the temple of God.*

64   2 Chronicles 9:1a *When the Queen of Sheba heard of Solomon's fame, she came to Jerusalem to test him with hard questions.*

65   2 Chronicles 12:1 *After Rehoboam's position as king was established and he had become strong, he and all Israel with him abandoned the law of the* LORD.

66   2 Chronicles 15:7 *But as for you, be strong and do not give up, for your work will be rewarded.*

Nathan Still a Gift of God

67   2 Chronicles 18 (Story of Jehoshaphat ignoring God's answer to his request.)

68   2 Chronicles 20:6 Jehoshaphat prayed to God and said: *"O Lord, God of our fathers, are you not the God who is in heaven? You rule over all the kingdoms of the nations. Power and might are in your hand, and no one can withstand you."*

69   2 Chronicles 28:22 *In his time of trouble King Ahaz became even more unfaithful to the Lord.*

70   2 Chronicles 32

71   2 Chronicles 32:7-8 *[7]Do not be afraid or discouraged because of the king of Assyria and the vast army with him, for there is a greater power with us than with him. [8]With him is only the arm of flesh, but with us is the Lord our God to help us and to fight our battles.*

72   Nehemiah 2:2-3: *[2]So the king asked me, "Why does your face look so sad when you are not ill? This can be nothing but sadness of heart." I was very much afraid, [3]but I said to the king, "May the king live forever! Why should my face not look sad when the city where my fathers are buried lies in ruins, and its gates have been destroyed by fire?"* Nehemiah 4:9: *But we prayed to our God and posted a guard day and night to meet this threat.*

73   Esther 1

74   Esther 6:1-2 *[1]That night the king could not sleep; so he ordered the book of the chronicles, the record of his reign, to be brought in and read to him. [2]It was found recorded there that Mordecai had exposed Bigthana and Teresh, two of the king's officers who guarded the doorway, who had conspired to assassinate King Xerxes.*

75   *Life Application Bible*, New International Version, (Wheaton, Illinois: Tyndale House Publisher's, Inc. and Grand Rapids, Michigan: Zondervan Publishing House, 1991), 840.

76   Isaiah 30:15 *This is what the Sovereign Lord, the Holy One of Israel, says: "In repentance and rest is your salvation, in quietness and trust is your strength, but you would have none of it.*

77   *Life Application Bible*, New International Version, (Wheaton, Illinois: Tyndale House Publisher's, Inc. and Grand Rapids, Michigan: Zondervan Publishing House, 1991), 888.

78   Lamentations 3:22-26, 31-32 [22]*Because of the Lord's great love we are not consumed, for his compassions never fail.* [23]*They are new every morning; great is your faithfulness.* [24]*I say to myself, "The Lord is my portion; therefore I will wait for him."* [25]*The Lord is good to those whose hope is in him, to the one who seeks him;* [26]*it is good to wait quietly for the salvation of the Lord.* [31]*For men are not cast off by the Lord forever.* [32]*Though he brings grief, he will show compassion, so great is his unfailing love.*

79   *Life Application Bible*, New International Version, (Wheaton, Illinois: Tyndale House Publisher's, Inc. and Grand Rapids, Michigan: Zondervan Publishing House, 1991), 895.

Chapter 13 Preparing for Transplant
80   Psalm 18:32-34: [32]*It is god who arms me with strength and makes my way perfect.* [33]*He makes my feet like the feet of a deer, he enables me to stand on the heights.* [34]*He trains my hands for battle; my arms can bend a bow of bronze.*

81   Psalm 20:6-8 [6]*Now I know that the Lord saves his anointed; he answers him from his holy heaven with the saving power of his right hand.* [7]*Some trust in chariots and some in horses, but we trust in the name of the Lord our God.* [8]*They are brought to their knees and fall, but we rise up and stand firm.*

82   Psalm 25:16-21: [16]*Turn to me and be gracious to me, for I am lonely and afflicted.* [17]*The troubles of my heart have multiplied; free me from my anguish.* [18]*Look upon my affliction and my distress and take away all my sins.* [19]*See how my enemies have increased and how fiercely they hate me!* [20]*Guard my life and rescue me; let me not be put to shame, for I take refuge in you.* [21]*May integrity and uprightness protect me, because my hope is in you.*

83   Psalm 27:1-3: [1]*The Lord is my light and my salvation-- whom shall I fear? The Lord is the stronghold of my life-- of whom shall I be afraid?* [2]*When evil men advance against me to devour my flesh, when my enemies and my foes attack me, they will stumble and fall.* [3]*Though an army besiege me, my heart will not fear; though war break out against me, even then will I be confident.*

84   Psalm 27:13-14: ¹³I am still confident of this: I will see the goodness of the Lord in the land of the living. ¹⁴Wait for the Lord; be strong and take heart and wait for the Lord.

85   Psalm 40:1-4: ¹I waited patiently for the LORD; he turned to me and heard my cry. ²He lifted me out of the slimy pit, out of the mud and mire; he set my feet on a rock and gave me a firm place to stand. ³He put a new song in my mouth, a hymn of praise to our God. Many will see and fear and put their trust in the LORD. ⁴ Blessed is the man who makes the LORD his trust, who does not look to the proud, to those who turn aside to false gods.

86   Psalm 46:1-3: ¹God is our refuge and strength, an ever-present help in trouble. ²Therefore we will not fear, though the earth give way and the mountains fall into the heart of the sea, ³though its waters roar and foam and the mountains quake with their surging.

87   Psalm 47:2 How awesome is the Lord Most High, the great King over all the earth!

88   Psalm 48:12-14: ¹²Walk about Zion, go around her, count her towers, ¹³consider well her ramparts, view her citadels, that you may tell of them to the next generation. ¹⁴For this God is our God for ever and ever, he will be our guide even to the end.

89   Psalm 56:3-4: ³When I am afraid, I will trust in you. ⁴In God, whose word I praise, in God I trust; I will not be afraid. What can mortal man do to me?

90   Psalm 62:1-2, 5-8: ¹My soul finds rest in God alone; my salvation comes from him. ²He alone is my rock and my salvation; he is my fortress, I will never be shaken. ⁵Find rest, O my soul, in God alone; my hope comes from him. ⁶He alone is my rock and my salvation; he is my fortress, I will not be shaken. ⁷My salvation and my honor depend on God; he is my mighty rock, my refuge.⁸ Trust in him at all times, O people; pour out your hearts to him, for God is our refuge. Selah

91   Psalm 66:10-12: ¹⁰For you, O God, tested us; you refined us like silver. ¹¹You brought us into prison and laid burdens on our backs. ¹²You let men ride over our heads; we went through fire and water, but you brought us to a place of abundance.

Appendix and Endnotes

92   Psalm 84:5-7: *⁵Blessed are those whose strength is in you, who have set their hearts on pilgrimage. ⁶As they pass through the Valley of Baca, they make it a place of springs; the autumn rains also cover it with pools. ⁷They go from strength to strength, till each appears before God in Zion.*

93   Psalm 89:24: *My faithful love will be with him, and through my name his horn will be exalted.*

94   Psalm 94:17-19: *¹⁷Unless the Lord had given me help, I would soon have dwelt in the silence of death. ¹⁸When I said, "My foot is slipping," your love, O Lord, supported me. ¹⁹When anxiety was great within me, your consolation brought joy to my soul.*

95   Psalm 95:8 *do not harden your hearts as you did at Meribah, as you did that day at Massah in the desert.*

96   Psalm 102:6-7: *⁶I am like a desert owl, like an owl among the ruins. ⁷I lie awake; I have become like a bird alone on a roof.*

97   Psalm 78:71-72: *⁷¹from tending the sheep he brought him to be the shepherd of his people Jacob, of Israel his inheritance. ⁷²And David shepherded them with integrity of heart; with skillful hands he led them.*

98   Psalm 106:2: *Who can proclaim the mighty acts of the Lord or fully declare his praise?*

99   Psalm 107:32: *Let them exalt him in the assembly of the people and praise him in the council of the elders.*

100   *Life Application Bible*, New International Version, (Wheaton, Illinois: Tyndale House Publisher's, Inc. and Grand Rapids, Michigan: Zondervan Publishing House, 1991), 1026.

101   Psalm 114:7 *Tremble, O earth, at the presence of the Lord, at the presence of the God of Jacob.*

102   Psalm 115:12 *The Lord remembers us and will bless us; He will bless the house of Israel, he will bless the house of Aaron.*

103   Psalm 116:3-4: ³*The cords of death entangled me, the anguish of the grave came upon me; I was overcome by trouble and sorrow. ⁴Then I called on the name of the Lord: "O Lord, save me!"*

104   *Life Application Bible*, New International Version, (Wheaton, Illinois: Tyndale House Publisher's, Inc. and Grand Rapids, Michigan: Zondervan Publishing House, 1991), 1034.

105   Psalm 118:8 *It is better to take refuge in the Lord than to trust in man.*

106   *Life Application Bible*, New International Version, (Wheaton, Illinois: Tyndale House Publisher's, Inc. and Grand Rapids, Michigan: Zondervan Publishing House, 1991), 1035.

107   Ibid., 1036.

108   Ibid., 1031.

Chapter 16 Life Goes On
109   Psalm 145:14 *The Lord upholds all those who fall and lifts up all who are bowed down.*

110   Psalm 147:5 *Great is our Lord and mighty in power; his understanding has no limit.*

111   Jeremiah 29:4-5 ⁴*This is what the Lord Almighty, the God of Israel says to all those I carried into exile from Jerusalem to Babylon:* ⁵*"Build houses and settle down; plant gardens and eat what they produce."*

Chapter 18 Journey Into Grief
112   Ezekiel 37:1-5 *The hand of the* LORD *was upon me, and he brought me out by the Spirit of the* LORD *and set me in the middle of a valley; it was full of bones.* ²*He led me back and forth among them, and I saw a great many bones on the floor of the valley, bones that were very dry.* ³*He asked me, "Son of man, can these bones live?" I said, "O Sovereign* LORD, *you alone know."* ⁴*Then he said to me, "Prophesy to these bones and say to them, 'Dry bones, hear the word of the* LORD*!* ⁵*This is what the Sovereign* LORD *says to these bones: I will make breath enter you, and you will come to life.*

113   *Life Application Bible*, New International Version, (Wheaton, Illinois: Tyndale House Publisher's, Inc. and Grand Rapids, Michigan: Zondervan Publishing House, 1991), 1913.

Chapter 19 God at Work
114   *Life Application Bible*, New International Version, (Wheaton, Illinois: Tyndale House Publisher's, Inc. and Grand Rapids, Michigan: Zondervan Publishing House, 1991), 1179.

115   Ibid., 1179.

Chapter 30 Time Goes On
116   T. D. Jakes, Editor, *Holy Bible, Woman Thou Art Loosed Edition,* New King James Version, (Nashville, Tennessee: Thomas Nelson Publishers, Inc., 1998), 379.

117   Ibid., 381.

118   Ibid., 815.

119   Ibid., 1069.